Checked 13/03/11 JH
Latest edn

603784

636·15

91
92
93
94
96
97
8

Flat Race Riding

WARWICKSHIRE COLLEGE OF AGRICULTURE

*D1460473

003784

Flat Race Riding

John Hislop

J. A. Allen
London

WARWICKSHIRE COLLEGE
LIBRARY

Class No:
636.151

Acc No:
00501859

British Library Cataloguing in Publication Data

Hislop, John
The theory and practice of flat race riding
1. Horse-racing
I. Title
798.4'3   SF334

ISBN 0–85131–434–1

© John Hislop 1987

No part of this book may be reproduced, stored in a retrieval system, or transmitted, in any form or by any means, electronic, mechanical, photocopying, recording or otherwise, without the written permission of the publishers. All rights reserved.

Published in Great Britain in 1987 by
J. A. Allen & Company Limited,
1, Lower Grosvenor Place, Buckingham Palace Road,
London, SW1W 0EL

Book production Bill Ireson

Printed in Great Britain

Contents

List of Illustrations

Preface

This book had its origins in articles I wrote for *The British Racehorse* during the 1970s. That magazine published a collection of the articles in a pamphlet which soon sold out and was not reprinted. Following continued enquiries for copies, J. A. Allen & Company Limited approached me to revise and update my earlier pamphlet. This I have now done and I have taken the opportunity to add more photographs and to expand the text. It also seems appropriate to include, by arrangement with the Jockey Club, an appendix on the use of the whip.

Acknowledgements

I am indebted to Professor C. W. Ottaway, Ph.D., F.R.C.V.S., of the Department of Veterinary Anatomy at Bristol University and to Professor P. R. Davis, Ph.D., M.B., B.S., F.I.Biol., of the Department of Human Biology at Surrey University, for their help.

For the figures, which are drawn from action photographs, I thank Professor J. R. Skeaping, R.A.

I would also like to thank all those whose knowledge and experience have enabled me to write this book, particularly the greatest of all producers of jockeys, the late Stanley Wootton.

All jockeys make mistakes, good jockeys make fewest

HARRY WRAGG

The test of a good jockey isn't the races he wins that he should win; it's the ones he wins that he shouldn't win

CHARLIE SMIRKE

Introduction

While there are many books on various other branches of equitation, flat race riding has been neglected almost entirely. Not many people have studied the principles affecting the art; and as a result, except in stables managed by one of the few trainers (most famous of all time being Stanley Wootton) with a flair for teaching apprentices, flat race riding instruction is haphazard – sometimes incorrect – and lads have to learn as best they can. Usually this consists in copying jockeys whom they admire or who are having a run of success, regardless of whether this is gained in spite of the way the jockeys ride, rather than because of it.

In addition, the average boy is born without horse-sense, has little or no opportunity of acquiring it during childhood and, due to a late school leaving age and shortage of labour in racing stables, is hurried through his riding education.

Moreover, many boys simply do not possess the attributes necessary to making good riders, any more than tone-deaf people can become good musicians.

In learning any skill, the first step is to understand thoroughly what it requires.

The keystone of flat racing, as of any aspect of equitation, is the horse itself. It is essential, therefore, to know how he functions, just as it is necessary for a racing-car driver to understand the working of the internal combustion engine.

Racehorses are sensitive creatures, who react to the way they are treated, both in and out of the stable. They are not markedly intelligent, but have good memories – I know of one horse who had been given some hard races by a jockey and would chase him out of the box whenever the jockey came visiting the stud where the horse now stood.

In character and temperament racehorses vary, as do people, and it is important to appreciate this. Treatment which works wonders with one horse may have the opposite effect on another.

Like that of people, the behaviour of horses depends upon their individual natures – whether they are nervous, bold, quick-tempered, phlegmatic and so on, and upon the way they have been brought up. Thus, a jockey will have to cope with horses who need delicate or strong handling, and those who have acquired undesirable habits as a result of bad upbringing.

Therefore to be able to deal with situations which may arise, the jockey should be a reasonably good horseman.

One of the elementary mistakes in approaching the art of flat race riding is the failure to appreciate that it comprises two separate skills, horsemanship and jockeyship.

Horsemanship is the ability to manage horses from the saddle. That is to say, not fall off; make them go in the desired direction; keep them balanced and on a true course; control their speed; stop them when required and make them happy in their work.

This entails a secure seat, good hands, physical fitness, sensitivity, confidence, understanding horses and knowing how to deal with the various aspects of their behaviour.

Jockeyship is the art of race riding – judgement of pace, tactics, sizing up the way a race is being run and acting accordingly, quickness from the start, riding a finish, determination and gamesmanship.

If the highest skill in flat race riding is to be attained, it is essential to master the art of horsemanship before attempting to be a jockey.

It is said, not without truth: "You can sometimes make a jockey out of a horseman, never a horseman out of a jockey."

This means that if anyone has got into the habit of riding the wrong way it is extremely difficult to get out of it; and that however good a jockey a man may be, he will never reach the highest standard if he is not a horseman as well.

With jockeys as with racehorses, success is largely relative. A moderate horse may sweep the board in a bad year and a jockey can appear outstanding in an era of sub-standard riders. For example, in the decade following the Second World War a run of success in amateur flat races came my way, which in pre-war days would have been impossible, because the class of riding then was so much higher than it was immediately after 1945.

A jockey should be judged by the way he fulfils the requirements of his profession, rather than by comparison with his contemporaries.

The education of a flat race jockey comes in two stages. The first is learning to be a horseman, the second learning to be a jockey. Not until he is reasonably proficient in the first stage should a prospective jockey be allowed to attempt the second.

The trouble at the present time is that circumstances only too often result in the first stage being rushed, neglected or wrongly imparted. As a result, boys often end up neither horsemen nor jockeys. So far as many trainers are concerned, they have "x" horses to get out at exercise and "y" riders available; and the problem of relating the one to the other becomes more important than that of teaching boys to ride well. Their first objective therefore is, merely, to bring boys as soon as possible to a stage where there is a reasonable chance of their getting up the canter without falling off or the horse running away with them. Other niceties of riding have to go by the board.

If a boy has been well taught before he arrives in a stable, is intelligent, resourceful, observant and ambitious – or a genius – he will teach himself and, sooner or later, make a competent jockey. Otherwise, he will either get nowhere, or, if he reaches the status of a jockey, will never attain the highest proficiency, because he will have developed ineradicable faults or lack at least one of the skills required to reach this standard.

The instruction in basic horsemanship available throughout Great Britain at the present time is good. It is also within the reach of a greater proportion of the community than was the case between the two wars. The Pony Club has done much to help, as have the many reputable riding schools which have sprung up due to the increasing popularity of equitation.

A number of trainers wisely send their apprentices to a riding school where they can be taught the first principles. This ensures that they start the right way, and lays the foundation of a good style, giving them a sense of balance, helping them to acquire sensitive hands and security in the saddle, and teaching them the fundamentals of controlling and managing horses.

Every form of riding consists in making the horse do a particular task, and whatever the nature of this task, it is necessary to have the horse under control – to be able to guide him, turn him, stop him, balance him, regulate his speed and help him to put his heart into his work.

Flat racing is no exception. The methods necessary to get the best results from a horse in a flat race are basically the same as those required in every branch of riding. They differ only in degree and in the adaptations necessary to particular circumstances. When such adaptations are taken to extremes, which interfere with the efficiency of the rider in carrying out any of the essential requirements of the task, they are a hindrance and not a help.

For instance, at racing pace, riding with long stirrup leathers makes it difficult to hold or balance a horse or to place the rider's weight so that it can be carried most easily and cut wind-resistance. Stirrup leathers which are too short deprive the rider of the full use of his legs, thus hindering him in keeping a straight course if the horse is hanging, or urging him forward without using the whip. It endangers his security in the saddle – you won't win if you fall off in the race – and tends to unbalance a horse through the rider's body being too high above the horse, where a slight movement has a greater effect on equilibrium than if he is close to the saddle.

The most effective seat is that which best fulfils all the requirements of the task.

No flat race jockey can afford to disregard any of the skills necessary to his profession. If he has a weakness in one of them, sooner or later it will find him out – it might cost him a Derby. And when a rival of equal ability in other respects, but without this weakness, appears on the scene – it will only be a matter of time before one does – the rival will always be at an advantage.

Therefore the first aspect to be considered is that of basic horsemanship.

1 Basic Horsemanship

Basic horsemanship, which is the foundation of flat racing as much as any form of riding, consists in making the horse do what is required of him, smoothly, unobtrusively and effectively.

It entails a secure seat, which in turn depends upon balance and grip. Further influences operating are the individual peculiarities of the horse, his equipment – type of bit, martingale, etc. – and the nature of the work he has to do. Also bearing upon it are such aspects as the relationship between horse and rider, knowledge of the psychology of horses and the fruits of practical experience.

A good flat racing seat is merely the modification of a good seat for general riding. At least, the rider's back should be straight, but not stiff; he should sit comfortably in the middle of the saddle; have his knees close to the horse and let the lower legs hang down naturally. The feet should rest naturally in the irons, pointing straight to the front – developing the habit of sticking the toes out can lead to catching them on an upright. Whether a rider has his feet inside or outside of the irons is a matter of personal taste. Riding with the feet on the inside of the irons tends to keep the lower leg closer to the horse and the toes from sticking out.

The length of stirrup leather depends upon: (a) how hard the horse pulls, (b) how fast he is required to go, (c) the way a horse gallops and (d) the build of the rider.

Theoretically, the length of the stirrup leather should be altered according to circumstances. If a horse who does not pull is only going to canter, there is nothing to be gained by riding short on him. If he is going to canter first and gallop afterwards, the correct theoretical procedure is to start out with reasonably long leathers and pull them up before galloping.

Likewise, if a horse has an extravagant, bounding stride, it is usually desirable to ride shorter on him than on a horse who has a short scrappy stride. One is better balanced riding shorter in a sprint race than in a long distance race.

In practice, most jockeys ride the same length at all times, because they have got into the habit of doing so, or cannot be bothered to alter their leathers once they have adjusted them.

While riding the same length under all circumstances saves trouble, it does not necessarily enable the greatest advantage to be gained, because it is a case of fitting the circumstances to the convenience of the rider, instead of the rider adapting himself to circumstances, thus making the most of the horse.

My experience is that a variation of a hole or two can increase efficiency to an appreciable extent.

The most effective length of rein for any type of riding is dependent upon prevailing conditions and the peculiarities of individual horses. Length of rein should not be too short to allow for a measure of play between the horse's mouth and the rider's hands, nor too long to prevent the rider being able to exercise full control. A good general guide when cantering or galloping is to have the hands level with the martingale strap.

The hands should be held low, just above or level with the horse's withers. A rider looks neater with his elbows in, especially if he has long arms, but several good jockeys rode with them stuck out.

A well-broken, good-mannered horse is not difficult to ride, because he answers to the aids. He will go forward, back, passage (move sideways), half-passage, turn, stop and regulate his pace according to the movements of the rider's hands and legs and word of command.

With the introduction of starting-stalls a jockey's task at the start has been simplified.

Still, not every race is started from stalls, while horses have to be ridden at home. And, if they are allowed to develop bad mouths and bad habits at home, horses are liable to become commensurately difficult to ride and, consequently, are less effective on the racecourse.

I have known horses become so unmanageable that they could

Plate 1 (left)
The late Steve Donoghue on The Tetrarch. One of the greatest jockeys of the present century, Donoghue was champion for ten successive seasons and rode four Derby winners, three off the reel, against extremely strong competition. A superb horseman, he rode with medium-short leathers customary at that time.

Plate 2 (below)
The late Manny Mercer on Darius. Manny, the best stylist since the war, rode before the fashion of ultra-short leathers came in.

Plate 3
Joe Mercer on Kris, giving a perfect example of the present day English style not carried to extremes. His weight is correctly disposed; his back is straight; his body is low enough to reduce wind resistance to a minimum, but enabling forward vision to be maintained; he has perfect contact with the horse's mouth; he is swinging the whip with economy, balance and effect – parallel with and close to the horse and in the correct hand, there being no horse on his off side. His feet are "home" in the stirrups in traditional English style, which is necessary if the lower part of the rider's leg is to be used for propulsion or guidance.

not be trained or raced, but when put right by intelligent handling won races.

While horse-breaking and the rehabilitation of intractable horses is not the primary duty of a jockey, it is a help to know something of this aspect of the business.

To start with, it is important to have an elementary knowledge of the psychology of horses. By nature they are gregarious. This trait is evident when a horse refuses to leave the string, or to turn away from the field out hunting. But if horses are required to do any task it is important that they understand discipline. If they are undisciplined, inconvenience, waste of time and accidents ensue.

The way a horse is broken and ridden in the early stages of his career can make or mar him; and those who ride racehorses often find themselves reaping the errors of others.

Horses who have been badly handled can be difficult or even impossible to cope with in ordinary circumstances, but at least it is a help to have some idea of how to approach the problem.

The usual method of dealing with a nappy horse in racing stables is for the head-lad or trainer to give him a couple round the hocks with the "Long Tom". This may serve to produce a temporary cure, but usually it will only be effective while the man with the Long Tom is within striking distance. As soon as the horse thinks he is out of range he is liable to play up again.

The only way to instil discipline in a horse is for him to respect the person riding him. And the only way to imbue this respect is for the rider to give the horse three or four real good cracks, hitting well behind the stifle, preferably with the left hand. Horses can sometimes be reformed by re-breaking them, but these measures are usually only necessary in extreme cases.

It is essential to realise another natural tendency in horses. This is, when they whip round, run off the canter, or in any other way deviate from a straight line, in 99 cases out of 100 they go to the left and not the right. This phenomenon cannot be too strongly stressed, because repercussions from it occur again and again on the racecourse, in the form of races lost, objections, interference and accidents due to horses going off to the left. Not infrequently they are encouraged to do so by the rider having his whip in the right hand.

Thus, not only should horses almost always be chastised left-handed, but they are more likely to run straight in a race when the jockey uses his whip left-handed rather than right-handed.

Therefore it is necessary for a jockey to be able to use the whip with either hand and essential that he can do so with his left hand, if he is to be considered master of his profession.

Using a whip in the unaccustomed hand, whether this is the right or left, is purely a matter of practice. When I went into a racing stable I could not use my left hand at all; but, by incessant practice, on and off a horse, I became virtually ambidextrous.

It is a help to use the unaccustomed hand as much as possible in everyday use, from cleaning one's teeth to carrying suitcases.

The same goes for twirling the whip through the fingers and pulling it through from one hand to the other. A jockey who is not fluent with the whip in either hand is not master of his trade, being equivalent to a tennis player who cannot play backhand shots or a cricketer who cannot hit bowling on the leg side.

Security of seat, balance and good hands go together. If a jockey does not possess the first two qualities he cannot acquire the third, since he will be relying on the reins to keep himself in position. Thus he will be exerting on the horse's mouth pressure

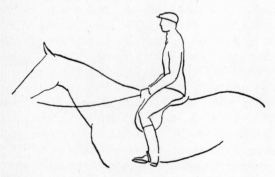

Figure 1.1
Seat for basic horsemanship

which is neither necessary nor indicative of any requirement.

If such pressure is exerted violently or unevenly, the horse will soon develop an insensitive or one-sided mouth. At the same time, it will confuse him as to what aids are being imparted to him.

The most effective methods of acquiring balance and security are, first, riding without reins and stirrups and, second, jumping both with and without reins and stirrups.

When reasonable proficiency in the art of basic horsemenship has been attained, it is an easy matter for a rider to adapt his seat to race riding, but far more difficult to reverse the process.

A well-schooled horse is like a perfectly running car: he answers to the slightest movement of the rider and unless the indications (aids) are given incorrectly the desired result will be produced.

The aids consist of the pressure of the rider's legs against the horse's sides, the pull of the reins on his mouth and their pressure against his neck. In the case of a well-schooled horse the aids need to be applied only gently; with an unschooled horse they will convey almost nothing.

Anyone who rides a horse regularly and is a good rider can get him going properly after a time. For example, one of the advantages of training and riding in France is that, owing to the chief training grounds being close to the Paris racecourses, a jockey has time to ride out regularly before he goes racing. As that

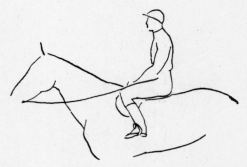

Figure 1.2
Seat for exercise riding and general purpose racing – flat, fences or hurdles

great jockey Charlie Elliott put it: "You can get to know a horse so well you become part of him."

This is worth much in the case of difficult horses, or those who have been badly broken, as a jockey – provided he is a good horseman – can repair the damage of bad handling and get a horse going smoothly and obediently.

2 *Riding at Exercise*

Exercise riding is quite different to race riding, but it is an unavoidable stage in becoming a jockey and an integral part of the profession.

The chief difference between exercise riding and race riding is that of tempo. On the training ground most work is carried out at a steady pace, and when horses gallop they are seldom off the bit. On the racecourse, horses are galloping at a degree faster from the start and, usually, are off the bit some way before the finish.

From the time a jockey is put up on a horse for a race to the time he returns to the paddock is only a few minutes. During this period the horse's attention is centred on the job at hand and, unless he is wayward by nature, nervous, green or startled, he rarely gives any trouble.

At exercise the rider is on the horse's back for up to two hours, unless he is out purely in the capacity of a work-rider. The horse has not the major purpose of a race upon which to fix his attention and sometimes is either bored by, or displeased with, the period of exercise. He may express his feelings in various ways. If indolent, he will be unwilling to take hold of his bit in any gait and, even in a stripped gallop, will be content to slouch along lengths behind the horses working with him.

Alternately, he may amuse himself by trying to get rid of his rider, refusing to go on to the working ground, running off it, taking a grab at the horse nearest to him or trying to go twice as fast as his rider wishes.

All this can prove disconcerting to the man on his back, as well as holding up the morning's work.

A good horseman should be able to adapt himself to the circumstances demanded by the type of riding in which he is participating. That is to say, if he is riding fast work on a racehorse in the morning and a hack in the show-ring in the afternoon, he should be at home with the greatly differing length of leathers required by these separate branches of equitation.

To a lesser degree, the same applies to exercise riding. The length of leathers should be adapted to the individual peculiarities of the horse, as opposed to the rider acquiring the habit of riding a certain length, regardless of the characteristics of the horse or the exact nature of the work. The variation may be only slight, but it can make an appreciable difference to efficiency. For instance, on a hard-pulling horse who likes trying to get rid of his rider on the way up to the gallops, it is advisable to ride fairly long (by racing standards), to ensure staying on the horse's back until the time comes to do fast work. Then, it is advisable to pull up the leathers in order to be able to hold the horse.

A good, strong rider should be able to achieve the happy medium of riding sufficiently long to avoid falling off if the horse "puts in one" on the way to the gallop, and sufficiently short to enable him not to be run away with when doing fast work; but the run-of-the-mill rider is more than likely to be put on the floor through being caught unawares when riding too short, or to "go for the letters" up the gallop through riding too long. Imitation of fashion, rather than scientific evaluation, is the most powerful factor in the formation of style among stable-lads and jockeys.

A rider who cannot adapt himself to circumstances is not master of the art of equitation and the familiar plea of "I feel all wrong if I change my length" is an admission of incompetence or lack of adaptability.

On a horse not given to unseating habits, length of leather is more or less immaterial, so long as it does not interfere with the comfort of the horse or the efficiency of the rider's performance.

An old-timer once told me: "Our Governor always made us ride long at exercise, nearly the full length of the leg, and we hardly ever had a loose horse."

This is an extreme which, if carried to the extent of fast work, entails the rider sitting up like a mounted policeman or sawing at the horse's mouth, in order to hold him; but it illustrates the value of not riding too short if security in the saddle is to be preserved.

The chief objective in exercise riding is to get the horse to do his work calmly and smoothly; so that he does not mess about or knock his legs during the process, or worry and fail to eat up when he gets home. This is both a training and a riding problem. However skilled and sympathetic a rider may be, his influence on the horse can be overcome by bad training methods. But since this treatise deals only with the aspect of riding, that of training must be discounted here.

Horses are highly sensitive to the mood of their riders, and nervousness or fear in the occupant of the saddle is soon communicated to his mount. Thus, whatever a rider feels, he should try to convey an air of confidence and mastery to his horse.

Nothing stirs a horse up more than the rider taking a hold of his head long before he reaches the jumping off point of the gallop. It is one thing to approach the start with a rein so long and loose that control is sacrificed, quite another to have a stranglehold on the horse's mouth.

There are two methods of dealing with this problem. One, which is traditionally English, is to walk on to the gallop with a comparatively long rein and shorten it after jumping off; the other, which is typical of the Australian and American schools, is to shorten the rein to the required galloping length before jumping off and not alter it.

The first method requires a certain adroitness in changing one's hold, so that the horse does not get first run and "swallow the poker" while the new hold is being taken up, which a cunning, hard-puller may succeed in doing.

The second method entails shortening the rein with sufficient delicacy of touch to disguise from the horse the fact that he is about to jump off, so that he does not get stirred up before doing so.

The choice between these two methods is a matter of opinion; the successful employment of either depends upon skill in carrying out the manoeuvre. One method may be more effective with one horse, and vice versa.

No form of riding is wasted, however remote it may be from the branch in which the participant is mainly interested. Thus exercise riding is of value in race riding although it differs from it.

Any form of exercise riding helps to develop or improve horse-sense, control, balance, security of seat, style, judgement of pace and other attributes necessary in a race. For the dedicated such exercise thus becomes a period of interest and value which, for the disinterested or unintelligent, represents boredom or dislike.

To start with, both for the comfort of the horse and the rider's safety, it is advisable to ensure that the tack has been properly adjusted. While this is the responsibility of the lad who gets the horse ready, it is the rider – quite probably someone else – who will suffer if anything goes wrong: the saddle pressing down on the withers; the bit too low or too high in the mouth; the nose-band improperly adjusted; the bit or bridle chafing, the girths too loose; the martingale too short or too long. These are all items which can cause trouble.

Some horses blow themselves out when they are first girthed up, and though the girths may feel tight enough then, in half an hour's time they will be quite loose. Therefore it is important to try the girths again before cantering or galloping.

There is a great deal more to riding at exercise than merely following the horse in front, or getting from the start to finish of a gallop more or less in line with the accompanying horses.

The way a horse goes is a direct reflection of whoever has been riding him regularly. One of the chief factors influencing the way a horse goes, at all paces, is the rider's touch on the reins, generally referred to as "hands".

If the horse has a bad mouth – unless for dental or medical reasons – it is the outcome of bad hands. If he is whipping round to the left, it is because he has been allowed to get into the habit – probably through the rider always carrying his whip in his right hand, or allowing the horse to complete the full circle, instead of pulling him round the opposite way. If he runs back or plays up at the canter's end it may well be because he resents having a stranglehold put on his mouth before jumping off. Likewise, if a horse gets kicked out at exercise it may result from being allowed to approach too close to another horse. Or, if he grabs hold of the horse nearest to him, the stirrup-iron or a neighbouring rider's leg, it is probably due to lack of attention on the part of his rider.

Possession of good hands is a quality difficult to define. It consists in a light, level, sympathetic, elastic pressure, inspired by the brain and conveyed through the arms, wrists, fingers, reins and bit to the horse's mouth, and thence to the horse's brain.

Fitness, strength, skill and sensitivity come into it, but in the end the co-ordination – or the battle – is one of minds, that of the horse and that of the rider. As a result, the performance of each is directly affected by the mood of each, for mental attitude is quickly conveyed from one to the other, particularly from the rider to the horse. I have known horses black with sweat in a couple of minutes as a result of a different rider changing on to them.

In this meeting of minds, confidence, sympathy, determination, patience, courage and similar mental qualities are a strong, beneficial influence. Conversely, such less desirable forces as anger, impatience, distrust and fear have a bad effect. This applies to all branches of riding, including racing.

So, from the moment a lad gets on a racehorse in the yard, or a jockey mounts in the paddock, it is important that he tries to get on good terms with the horse, so that the horse will go smoothly and happily.

Whether on the working ground or going to the post, the same principles apply: making the horse set off calmly and smoothly; not pulling him about; keeping well clear of the horse in front; preserving an even pace; picking the best going and pulling up gradually – this is important because pulling up with a jerk may strain a tendon or ligament.

Anyone who has ridden out with a good stable before and after the Second World War, as I have done, will appreciate the steep drop in the standard of riding during the post-war period. The situation is much improved today due to the recent move to establish courses of riding instruction for apprentices.

That the riding standards of stable-lads in general has deteriorated so much since the war is due to many lads being given virtually no proper tuition. Owing to the shortage of labour in stables, trainers have had to push lads along too fast; so that they

Figure 2.1
Wrong way to ride a puller – short rein and longish leathers give little elasticity or power.

Figure 2.2
Correct way to ride a puller – medium length rein and short stirrups give elasticity with power.

have never had the chance to acquire the basic principles of riding and too often have formed ineradicable faults. At times it has just been a case of putting up a boy and hoping that he will get out and in without falling off or being run away with, regardless of anything else.

Most horses go best when ridden on a long rather than short rein; and when cantering or taking a horse down to the post, the longer the rein the better, provided it is compatible with control.

Occasionally a horse goes best when ridden on a short rein, which can only be found out by trial and error.

Likewise, holding hard-pullers is a matter of trial and error: my own experience is that, in general, the best method is to ride them with short leathers and a longish rein.

The more play that is given to a horse's mouth – as opposed to exerting a steady, dead pull – the more likely is he to go well. The play may be so delicate as to be almost imperceptible, but if it succeeds in getting the horse to ease the pressure on his bit, even fractionally, it is a help to holding him. Persuading the horse to lessen the hold on his bit, rather than trying to hold him by pure strength, is the key to the problem.

Horses will sometimes pull because they are afraid for their mouths and, when they realise that discomfort or pain is not going to ensue, cease to take hold.

Some years ago I used occasionally to ride a big, strong horse at exercise called By Thunder! (by Nearco-Vertencia, by Deiri), a hard-puller who won the Yorkshire Cup, Ebor Handicap and other races. Fortunately I discovered that by putting the little finger of my left hand in the neck-strap he became a different ride altogether: he settled down and took no more than a steady, racing hold.

In an endeavour to hold him, the lads had got into the way of pulling his head round to the right, doubtless because they were stronger in the right hand than in the left; and having a finger of the left hand on the neck-strap seemed more comfortable for him, giving him confidence and eliminating the desire to fight for his head.

Many horses go well ridden this way, possibly because,

27

automatically, the rider's hands are in the correct position and part of the pressure is on the neck-strap instead of the horse's mouth.

From the aspect of training, it is extremely important that a horse should not become upset before he works. If he tears up the cantering ground, being pulled here and there, not only has he done the equivalent of a gallop before he does fast work, but he may knock his legs about or strain a ligament or tendon through treading on bad going – it used to be a strict rule in our stable to keep your horse on the best going on the cantering ground, however narrow the strip.

To ensure that his horses always were ridden to his liking in their preliminary canter, the late Fred Darling made all his lads sit down in the saddle and ride with a long rein, the horses doing no more than hack-cantering. A jockey down to ride work was never put up until the preliminary canter had been completed, in case he upset the horse by getting hold of his head and sitting up his neck.

Training methods are dependent, among other factors, on racing methods. In America, where tracks are smaller than in Europe, and the average race shorter, early speed is of great importance. Therefore to train horses as if they were going to run over a mile-and-a-half or upwards in Europe, and ride them accordingly, would probably mean that they never got in the American race until it was over.

On the other hand, to train and ride an Ascot Gold Cup horse by American methods could result in the horse running himself to a standstill long before the finish.

When the American horse, Reigh Count, was brought over to race in England with the Ascot Gold Cup as his main objective, he first ran three times ridden by his usual American jockey, Chic Lang. Jumped off and sent along from the start, he failed to reach the first three.

It was then decided to have him ridden by an English jockey, using orthodox English tactics. With Joe Childs up, Reigh Count won the Coronation Cup at Epsom and, this time partnered by Harry Wragg, divided Invershin and Palais Royal II in the Ascot Gold Cup.

If a horse can be made to run relaxed during a race, without pulling and tearing, he has something left for the finish. So, unless he is naturally lazy, it is important to teach him to do this at home.

Even in a spring race this holds, because no horse can run at absolute top speed for more than about two furlongs. Naturally, it is more difficult to teach a sprinter, or a horse required to race under American conditions, to relax and be waited with, but it is not impossible.

Some years ago the late Atty Persse engaged an apprentice for a very short runner, who was always being beaten through fading in the last hundred yards. The boy's master had noticed this and told him not to jump the horse out of the gate, but to get him covered up and wait with him, whatever his riding instructions from Atty. Being in even greater awe of his master than of Atty, who told him to jump off and go all the way, the boy obeyed the former who had a good bet on the horse, which won.

It is important for horses to be ridden at home in such a way as to encourage them to go as required in a race. Thus a jockey riding a horse with a good chance of winning important engagements usually is keen to ride him in his fast work at home, to get him going to his liking and establish a mutual confidence and understanding, which will be a valuable asset on the racecourse.

Getting a horse to relax during the exercise gallop or a race is dependent upon good hands, confidence between horse and rider, and the way in which he is worked.

Half the battle is to persuade the horse to jump off calmly and steadily. It is only too easy, as a rule, to put him into top gear and make him take a strong hold of his bit; but if he jumps off at full pressure the chances are that he will get first run on the rider, who will never be able to settle him.

The best way to get horses to settle is to set them off in single file, remaining thus till the last couple of furlongs and then moving upsides and finishing in line. This has the added advantage of teaching horses that the time when they are required to go fastest is at the end of the race.

The worst way for horses to go is for them to tear away too fast at the start and get slower and slower. This is especially damaging if horses are unfit, since it imposes a great strain on heart, lungs, tendons and ligaments, also causing the horse to lose his action, sprawl and perhaps hit himself.

With very lazy horses, even stayers, it is a different matter. Often they do best when their fast work is confined to five or six furlongs, upsides. This was brought out in Doug Smith's autobiography, when he was writing about that great stayer, Alycidon, a very difficult horse to train on account of his extreme idleness.

All this is a matter of training rather than riding, but it is important for a jockey to appreciate the principles, in order to understand fully the nature of his task.

A good work-rider is worth much to a trainer, as he enables the most to be made of horses.

Once the horse has jumped off, the rider can take up a shorter hold – unless he has done so before walking on to the gallop. From then on, the quieter he sits and the less he pulls the horse about, the better.

Throughout the gallop, the horse should be on an even keel, negotiate corners leading with the correct leg, avoid zig-zagging about the gallop, hanging into other horses or striking into their heels. At the finish he should be pulled up gradually and trotted well out.

A vital factor in work-riding, as on the racecourse, is judgement of pace. In England, where conditions vary so much on different courses and training grounds, as well as with the prevailing going, judgement of pace is more a matter of instinct than of the clock. A fast time in one set of circumstances might represent a slow one in another, and vice versa.

Judgement of pace is thus as much a matter of experience and sensitivity as of mechanical timing, though being able to ride to the clock, where consistent conditions allow the most to be made of this skill, is a valuable asset.

3 The Flat Racing Seat

The average flat race jockey, if asked to expound the principles upon which he bases his style of riding, would be unlikely to produce a lucid, rational answer.

No scientific study has been made of the subject, and most jockeys have formed their style on the trends of fashion, or acquired it as much by accident as by design.

That great American flat race rider, Eddie Arcaro, once told me that he only rode "acey-deucy" (the off stirrup several holes shorter than the near side one) because, when he first entered a racing stable, the leading jockeys rode this way, so he copied them.

When the modern style of flat race riding, as opposed to that embodying ultra-long stirrup leathers and an upright body-carriage, was introduced at the beginning of this century, the advantage gained by those employing the new method was tremendous. But once the general principle of eliminating wind resistance and shifting the rider's weight forward, at the same time giving the horse's hindquarters greater freedom of action, had become standard practice among jockeys the effects of different styles became markedly reduced.

More telling were such factors as judgement in all aspects of race riding, balance, the ability to get horses to run generously, nerve, decisiveness and determination.

Thus it became and remains not uncommon for flat race riders with a bad style, but possessing to a high degree the other qualities necessary to good jockeyship, to produce better results than more technically correct opponents not so endowed. For instance, to take an extreme case, if a horse who has to be held up for a short run is brought to the front too soon, it is the tactical error, rather than a difference in the style of riding that is most likely to bring about his defeat.

Only when jockeys are exactly matched in all other ways is a difference in style likely to sway the balance; even then, the difference will have to be such that the faulty style is decidedly pronounced, before the scale is tipped between defeat and victory. His greatest admirers could not but admit that Sir Gordon Richards was no stylist, yet he remained a champion against all comers until his retirement in late middle age.

In the period between the First and Second World War, starting in the late-1920s, French jockeys used to ride appreciably shorter than their English counterparts – some of them not much longer than their successors of the present day – yet I cannot think of one approaching the class of such as Gordon Richards, Steve Donoghue, Charlie Smirke, Charlie Elliott and Brownie Carslake, to name some of the notable English riders of that day. When Elliott went to ride in France, for personal reasons of finance, he made his French counterparts look very moderate.

This suggests that, provided a jockey rides short enough for his horse to derive the benefits accruing from the general principles of the post-1900 style, there is nothing to be gained by riding shorter.

Further weight to this argument is given by the fact that such as George Moore, Scobie Breasley and Bill Williamson, riding an equivalent length to that used by Smirke and Elliott before the Second World War – both rode longer after the war, due doubtless to the advent of middle age and its attendant propensity to muscle-cramp – proved as effective, or more so, than the best protagonists of the present day ultra-short-stirrup school.

Riding with ultra-short stirrups imposes certain demands which are not in accordance with efficiency.

To start with, it decreases security in the saddle. This is less important than in steeplechasing but it should not be disregarded.

"You won't win if you don't get round" is one of the first principles of National Hunt racing and, even on the flat, unseating exigencies occasionally crop up during a race or on the way to the post.

Secondly, it lessens the effectiveness of the use of the lower part

Plate 4

Two good examples of modern riding. The jockey on number 8 is riding with his toes in the irons, American style, but his body is angled to enable him to see where he is going, as opposed to his face being buried in his horse's mane which is common with American jockeys, probably to avoid the dirt being flung up. He is riding too short to allow for him to kick the horse, so wisely is not trying to do so, thus avoiding the awkward and insecure positions liable to result from such an attempt when riding very short. His seat is just clear of the saddle: American jockeys usually sit closer to the horse than English jockeys, but even if actually in the saddle their weight is always well forward.

The jockey on number 10 is adopting a mixture of English and American styles. He is sitting down in the saddle, but his weight is well forward. His feet are "home" in the irons and his leathers are long enough to give him control and limited use of his legs in kicking the horse without loss of balance or displacement of weight.

Both jockeys have good contact with their horses' mouths, and number 8 has his whip in the correct hand: between him and the horse beside him.

Plate 5

A particularly interesting picture since the two jockeys are riding in styles of different eras. Number 4 is riding long, even by pre-war standards, yet his weight is actually further forward than that of number 2, which bears out the principle that, provided the leathers are short enough to enable the rider's weight to be correctly disposed for him to be properly balanced, and to enable him to hold the horse if he pulls, there is no practical advantage in riding any shorter. In fact, number 4 looks as if he would be better balanced and neater were he to be riding a bit shorter, as his seat is too high out of the saddle. That he has no contact with the horse's mouth is forgivable, since he is in a desperate finish at the winning post, when it is permissible and sometimes expedient to "give him the lot".

Number 2 is riding with ultra-short leathers and looks tidier, but it did not win him the race.

of the leg as an aid to control and propulsion, because it places it in a position in which active use of it is greatly restricted.

If a jockey attempts to use his legs vigorously when riding ultra-short, his weight is shifted to the wrong place and the risk of unbalancing the horse is increased.

Thus, in using the ultra-modern style, a rider must rely almost entirely on his hands, his whip, the pressure of his knees and that of his heels – as opposed to a more vigorous use of the lower part of the leg common to riding with longer leathers.

In favour of the ultra-short method is that the rider is sitting very still in the saddle and cannot irritate the horse by kicking him vigorously, even if he wishes to do so.

Against it, so far as riding a finish goes, is that in the case of a lazy horse who needs driving, but will not run on under the whip, the rider's scope is limited by the restricted use of the lower part of his leg.

An interesting finding emerges from the fact that many horses run on well when ridden in the ultra-modern style, even without the jockey recoursing to the whip. This is because, on the whole, the racehorse enjoys his task and is a willing partner in the operation, only too pleased to give of his best when his rider is doing no more than sitting still in a well-disposed position, moving his hands in rhythm with the horse, keeping contact with his mouth and generally going with him, instead of kicking him in the ribs, flapping the reins about, throwing his body backwards and forwards and, as they say, "going faster than the horse".

On the other hand, there is nothing to stop a jockey sitting quietly and going with his horse, without kicking him, when not riding with ultra-short leathers.

Furthermore, when riding with ultra-short stirrup leathers, a jockey is liable to muscle-cramp unless he raises his seat high in the saddle, because of the ensuing acute angle between the thigh and the shin bone. This applies particularly in long-distance racing; in a sprint race an acute angle between thigh and shin bone can be maintained throughout.

The higher the rider's body is above the horse, the more likely is any movement to upset his balance; and even a minor upset can hinder the horse's progress, perhaps representing the difference between defeat and victory.

There are so many factors to be considered in race riding that it is easy to confuse cause with effect.

For example, a jockey who rides ultra-short and sits absolutely still will be more effective than one who rides longer and "rocks the boat" – and vice versa.

But, all else being equal, the rider whose style is scientifically correct will always beat the one whose style is not.

The chief aims of the flat racing seat are:

(1) Not to fall off. Riding excessively short increases the danger of this. I can recall two cases of leading jockeys losing races (one a Group race) through falling off shortly before the winning post with the race at their mercy, as a result of overbalancing because they were riding too short.

(2) To place the rider's weight where it can be carried most easily. That is to say, in a position in which the rider's centre of gravity is exactly over that of the horse.

If the rider's centre of gravity is behind, or in front of that of the horse, it is in the wrong place. For the rider's centre of gravity to be in front of that of the horse, as opposed to behind it, is the lesser of two evils, especially if the horse is accelerating; but scientifically, this position is not so efficient as when the centre of gravity of the rider is exactly over that of the horse.

(3) To be able to guide, control, balance and urge forward the horse to the fullest effect, if necessary without using the whip, which some horses resent.

(4) To minimise wind resistance.

(5) To ensure adequate forward vision.

The positions of the centre of gravity of the rider and of the horse vary slightly with the movement of each during a race, but the area involved is comparatively small so that for all practical purposes it is the style of the jockey, rather than the length of the stirrup leathers, that determines the placing of the centre of gravity of the horse and that of the rider.

In Figure 3.1, where the jockey is riding short, but not ultra-

34

short, his centre of gravity is directly over that of the horse. He is sitting "against" the horse, as opposed to driving him. Had he been driving the horse, as is the jockey in Figure 3.2, the lower part of his leg would have been drawn back slightly and his knee would have come a little further forward.

In Figure 3.2 the jockey is riding longer than those riders in Figures 3.1, 3.3 and 3.4, but his centre of gravity is exactly over that of the horse.

The position is not academically perfect, because the jockey's seat is a little too high out of the saddle – the higher above the horse a jockey's seat, the easier it is for the horse to be thrown off balance – but Figure 3.2 is not an extreme case, so there is little danger of progress being adversely affected through the horse becoming unbalanced.

In Figure 3.3, where the jockey is riding ultra-short, his centre of gravity is a little ahead of that of the horse. The discrepancy could be overcome by the rider slightly lowering his seat, though this would render the angle between the thigh and shin bone so acute that the rider would be liable to muscle-cramp if he tried to maintain the position for any length of time.

In Figure 3.4 the jockey is riding with ultra-short stirrup leathers, at the same time sitting down in the saddle in order to make more use of the lower part of his legs. As a result of this horrible position, his centre of gravity is well behind that of the horse, thereby imposing an unnecessary burden on the horse.

Apart from the length of the stirrup leathers, the chief factors influencing style are the position of the back and the wrists.

The straighter the back, the closer to the horse will the rider sit and, in consequence, the better will be his balance.

Riding with a dead-straight back restricts the movement of the shoulders to some extent, so is more in keeping with the quiet style of riding a finish than the vigorous style; but those jockeys in which the straight backed style has been particularly marked have nearly always proved extremely effective, notably Scobie Breasley, George Moore and the late Manny Mercer. Incidentally, Manny Mercer rode with the orthodox length of stirrup leathers – long by ultra-modern standards – and apart from proving one of the best

Figure 3.1
A perfect position in the circumstances, that is to say, sitting against the horse as opposed to riding him out. The length of leathers is short enough to ensure proper balance at racing pace, but long enough to give control and security. The rider's seat is close to the saddle, but clear of it and his body is streamlined without loss of forward vision. The centre of gravity, ●, of the rider is directly over that of the horse.

Figure 3.2
An excellent position, except that the rider's seat is a little too high above the saddle. Here the jockey is scrubbing and his centre of gravity is exactly over that of his horse. His leathers are of a length compatible with balance, security and control; contact has been maintained with the horse's mouth and the body is streamlined, forward vision being maintained.

Figure 3.3
This jockey is riding with ultra-short leathers, and his centre of gravity is over that of his horse. Contact, streamlining and field of vision are in order, but he is riding too short to use his legs with effect as a means of propulsion or guidance, while any violent untoward movement on the part of the horse might result in a dissolution of the partnership.

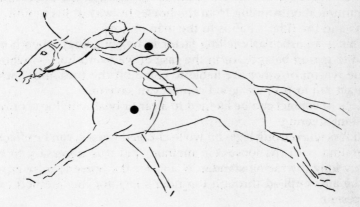

Figure 3.4
A horrible position. The jockey is trying to ride the horse out with hands and heels, but is riding so short that he has had to sit down in the saddle in order to give his legs more freedom of use. As a result, his centre of gravity is well behind that of his horse, so that progress is being achieved in spite of the rider's position rather than because of it. The extreme shortness of the leathers have brought the rider's knees above the withers, so that security and control are minimised.

jockeys to emerge after the Second World War he was one of the most stylish.

Whether a jockey rounds his shoulders, thereby slightly bending his back, or not, when riding a finish, the straighter he keeps his back throughout a race the better balanced is he likely to remain.

American jockeys, in general, sit much closer to their horses than do English jockeys. This may be due partially to their being smaller in build, on the whole, than those here, and to the "acey-deucy" style entailing riding longer on the near-side, than on the off-side. American jockeys in Europe usually ride level.

The way in which the wrists are held is more important than is generally appreciated. It affects the position of the elbows and the far more vital problem of maintaining contact with the horse's mouth.

The importance of contact is that it enables the rider to convey to the horse instantly any message pertaining to change of direction and speed, however slight, at the same time helping to balance him and give him a sense of confidence through the direct line of communication running from the horse, by way of his mouth, the reins and the rider's hands to the man on top.

This is a particularly telling factor in heavy going, when horses tend to get off balance, or in the case of wayward horses, who for some reason or other are liable to come off the true line. Lack of contact can lose a race, good contact can save one.

Lack of contact can be likened to a car or boat with loose or non-existent steering.

Riders with strong legs, on well-schooled horses, can be effective operating with the loose-rein method, but it is necessary to ride pretty long (by racing standards) and for the horse to answer well to the aids applied through the rider's legs for this method to be successful.

Contact does not mean taking a tight hold of the horse's mouth, but for the pressure to be sufficient to keep the rein taut, the weight of the pressure depending on such circumstances as how hard the horse pulls, how well he is going and whether he is hanging or running straight.

By keeping the wrists up as far as possible, in the position in which tennis players are taught to play forehand shots, it is easier to maintain contact than when holding them in any other manner.

Besides this, keeping the wrists up automatically brings the elbows closer to the body, resulting in streamlining and neatness of style.

For this hint, which helped appreciably to reduce the considerable room for improvement existing in my own flat racing style, I am indebted to the greatest of all mentors in the art of race riding, Stanley Wootton.

The length of rein depends upon individual taste, the style of the rider and the build and nature of the horse. As noted earlier, it can be varied according to the stage of the race or can be maintained at the same length throughout. My own principle was to ride with a longish rein during the race and shorten it when picking the horse up. The theory of this method being to encourage the horse to run relaxed until the time came for him to produce his maximum effort.

Every jockey holds his reins in a bridge, some using a double bridge (Figure 3.5), others a single bridge (Figure 3.6). This, again, is a matter of individual taste.

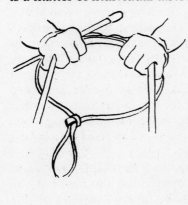

Figure 3.5
Reins held with a double bridge

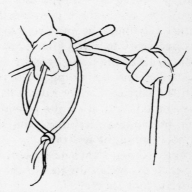

Figure 3.6
Reins held with a single bridge

The advantage of using a double bridge is that, if the rider starts with his hands fairly close together, he can shorten his hold in a fraction of a second by bringing them further apart and further up the horse's neck, at the same time allowing the slack to slip through the fingers.

It sounds a complicated procedure, but in fact is simple and automatic.

Some jockeys ride with the rein between the third and fourth fingers, others with the rein outside the little finger. My own preference is for the former style, as it seems to give a more sensitive touch.

South American jockeys ride with the rein between the thumb and first finger. I do not know the principles of the theory behind this style, but most South American jockeys are extremely good horsemen – much of their work is ridden without a saddle – both on and off the racecourse, so they must have good grounds for using this method.

In all aspects of racing, wind resistance is an important factor. Streamlining to diminish wind resistance and increase speed is an all-important influence in the design of cars, aeroplanes and boats, so must be respected when it comes to race riding. At the same time, it must be related to forward vision. This is essential on racecourses, such as Epsom and Brighton, where sticking to the rails all the way round results in going lengths further than is necessary.

Thus, while a jockey should tuck in his elbows and feet and keep his head low when there is no need for forward vision, as when fighting out a finish, he must be able to see where he is going when this is necessary to avoid giving away ground or to avoid striking into the heels of the horse in front.

A detail of flat race riding is the way in which the jockey's feet rest in the stirrups. Some ride with the foot on the inside of the stirrup, others with it on the outside. My preference was for the former method, as it brings the legs closer to the horse and prevents turning the feet out.

Recently some jockeys have been copying the American habit of riding with the ball of the foot or the toe taking the weight, instead of with the foot "home".

Plate 6
The "lavatory seat" position. The shortness of the leathers and the angle of the rider's body have placed his weight on the back of the saddle, well behind the centre of gravity, also offering too much wind resistance. (Compare this position with that of number 10 in Plate 4: both jockeys have their seats in the saddle, but number 10 has his weight forward and his body angled to reduce wind resistance.)

Plate 7

An American jockey riding in Europe. An excellent example of a tall jockey disposing himself, neatly, stylishly and effectively. In true American fashion his toes are in the irons, he is close to the horse, his crouch is low, but he can see ahead and he is riding short. His wrist is correctly angled, thereby keeping his elbows in. A jockey of this build is likely to get better results by sitting still, with short leathers, and riding his horse out with hands or whip, than by riding longer and using his legs, which might unbalance the horse.

Plate 8
The grotesque and hazardous position of number 11 is the result of trying to kick
a horse when riding with ultra-short leathers. It says much for the balance and
acrobatic skill of the rider that he is able to keep his horse running straight and
collected, maintain perfect contact with his mouth and win the race.

A less talented rider endeavouring to emulate this feat would probably fall off.
It is not an acceptable risk to make such an attempt, since a more orthodox style
would produce the same result.

Plate 9
The "war-whoop Red Indian" style of using the whip: ungainly, unbalanced and liable to cause the horse to swerve away from it; also, the rider has the whip in the wrong hand, running the risk of being penalised if his horse had bumped the other. As it was, the horse on the left won. (Compare this picture with Plate 3.)

Riding on the ball of the foot or toe gives more elasticity than riding with the foot "home", but is not so secure, as it makes it easier for the foot to get knocked out of the iron, than when the foot is "home".

If little or no use is to be made of the lower part of the leg in riding a finish, the ball-of-the-foot/toe method is admirable; but if a horse is to be kicked out vigorously, it is advisable to ride with the foot "home".

The elasticity resulting from the toe-in-the-iron style eases the leg muscles.

4 Tactics

In racing as in war, tactics begin before the contest takes place.

They depend, to start with, upon all information available concerning the horse, the going, the nature of the course, the strength and plans of the opposition; upon security and gamesmanship.

After that the factors affecting tactics are: riding orders; the start; the way the race is run; the manner in which the horse is going and any peculiarities he may possess; the tactics of the opposition and the unforeseen.

The more a jockey knows about the horse he is riding, the better his chance of success. How often does one hear remarks such as: "If only I'd ridden him before and known him, we'd have won."?

Information of value, sometimes essential to making the most of a horse, is:

(1) The type of going he likes.

(2) His best distance.

(3) Whether he is free or lazy.

(4) Whether he will run on under the whip, will not stand hitting or can only be hand-ridden.

(5) Whether he must be waited with, likes to go along or can be ridden any way, according to circumstances.

(6) The length of his finishing run.

(7) Any peculiarities of the horse, such as hanging, trying to savage other horses, being unwilling to pull out from behind other horses, nervousness at going through an opening.

(8) Dislike of being jostled or bumped.

(9) Having a resolute nature or a cowardly one.

(10) The state of his fitness.

It is extremely important to understand the powers or failings of horses in general, as well as of individual horses. A racehorse produces his optimum performance when his nervous energy is conserved until the moment the supreme effort is required. If he becomes unduly upset before a race, runs away going to the post or pulls and tears during the race, he will be a spent force by the finish.

Therefore it is highly desirable to keep him as calm as possible before a race and relaxed during the running of it.

Nor does the horse's system react favourably to sudden acceleration or change of direction, or to rough handling.

Some horses have a far higher rate of acceleration than others, and manoeuvreability varies greatly among different individuals. But the more suddenly a horse is asked to change his speed or move out of the line in which he is advancing, the more energy he is likely to lose and the more likely he is to become unbalanced.

Balance is a highly important quality in race riding. When a horse becomes unbalanced he is thrown out of his stride or caused to shorten it, which in terms of ground lost during a race can add up to lengths, representing a comparable loss of energy.

One of the most noticeable attributes of all great riders is that their horses are invariably perfectly balanced and running smoothly at all periods of the race, including the finish, however desperately it is being fought out – through unbalancing a horse in the last couple of strides, as a result of over-energetic riding, I dead-heated for a race which I ought to have won.

Hasty action should never be allowed precedence over balance, however critical the situation. A fraction of a second taken up in giving the horse an indication of what is required of him, before making a fresh move, ensures that he maintains his balance during a change of speed or direction and is time well spent. This is evident, especially, in National Hunt racing when a horse lands over the last obstacle. If he is given time to get on an even keel before being asked for a finishing effort, even if it means losing ground temporarily, he stands a far better chance of winning than if his rider starts kicking, scrubbing and using his whip, almost before the horse's forefeet have touched the ground. Two short-head victories under National Hunt rules, which otherwise undoubtedly would have gone against me, came my way through regarding this principle.

Theoretically, necessary information should be imparted by the trainer; but often it is not, perhaps through pressure of time, thoughtlessness or lack of the power of lucid expression. On one occasion my orders from the trainer for whom I was riding were so delphic that I left the paddock by no means certain whether the horse was fancied or not. Since the trainer appeared entirely gratified by our success, it can be presumed that the horse was "off".

The outline of tactics, apart from the trainer's instructions, can be drawn by referring to the horse's form. Scrutiny of this would show the type of going to which he is best suited, whether he is most effective if ridden from behind or going along, whether honest or irresolute and his best distance.

Next, much can be learnt from other jockeys who have ridden the horse previously, though it is advisable to make due allowance for their disseminating false information through ulterior motives – annoyance at having been taken off the horse, furthering the cause of their own mount in the race, and so on.

Breeding is another clue to a horse's behaviour; but it must be related to more tangible sources of evidence, because the genetic pattern offers so many permutations that the same pedigree can produce widely differing results.

One of the most delicate aspects of tactics is to decide if and when riding orders should be disregarded, owing to unforeseen circumstances.

Some trainers eliminate this problem by giving no orders at all, on the principle that rigid instructions tie a jockey down dangerously, as when the unforeseen occurs; so that by holding to a preconceived plan not suited to changed circumstances, instead of using his initiative, a jockey can lose the race.

An experienced jockey who knows the horse does not require any orders, but if a horse has a peculiarity of which the jockey is unaware it is helpful, often vital, to tell him about it.

A jockey is always well advised in the case of trainers who issue intricate and firm orders, to obtain leave to act contrary to instructions in case of emergency.

If a jockey is not capable of coping correctly with a tactical situation on his own initiative, the chances are that he is not capable of carrying out orders accurately. Asking a jockey to repeat back orders he has received can be illuminating, if not disturbing.

However, this is fundamentally a trainer's problem. The concern of the jockey is to perfect the skills necessary to tactics at the highest level, so that he has the confidence and ability to do the right thing at the right moment, by instinct.

One of the great attributes of a jockey is good tactical sense, with ability to appreciate a situation almost before it has developed and take the correct action instantly.

While to some extent this is a gift, it is also the fruit of assiduous study of the subject, alertness, concentration and learning from experience, all of which can be acquired by determination and attention to the job.

Security is an aspect which is often overlooked and, on the Turf as in war, neglect of it can bring disaster. Lack of security was largely responsible for the costly failure of the Dieppe raid in the Second World War, and a comparable leakage of riding plans can end by playing into an opponent's hands.

Such items of information as a horse being short of work, or that the jockey is or is not going to make running, if percolating into the enemy camp can give him a tactical advantage which may turn defeat into victory. The less information that is disseminated to the opposition, the stronger the tactical position.

From the moment a jockey is put on the horse in the paddock, the tactical situation begins to unfold.

If the horse is nervous or highly strung, he must be kept as calm as possible. It is advisable to avoid being chased on the way down to the post, or to let the horse jump off upsides another and dash off as if the race was on. Hard-pulling horses are best taken down last, steadily and away from others, or behind a placid horse who is going down slowly.

If the journey to the post involves going round a bend, it is often prudent to keep to the outside rail, since horses associate the inside with racing.

Lazy horses, on the other hand, will benefit from being woken up, sometimes with a couple of slaps, and made to stride along at a good half-speed for a couple of furlongs.

Trainers differ on how a horse should be taken down to the post. Their views usually depend upon the nature of the horse and whether or not he has worked on the morning of the race.

Like cars, horses run most efficiently when the engine has been warmed up. If a horse's circulation is going well and his limbs are loosened he will race better and achieve his maximum potential quicker than if his circulation and action are sluggish.

One horse I used to ride, so his trainer discovered, was never any good unless he did a fast couple of furlongs on the morning of the race.

While this aspect, primarily, is one of training it concerns the jockey greatly, because it can make the difference between winning and losing. Therefore it is a help to know what work, if any, the horse has done on the morning of the race, and in the absence of explicit instructions from the trainer to act accordingly.

If the horse has had a good pipe-opener in the morning, it should be unnecessary to give him another on the way to the post. But if he has not had a pipe-opener before racing and is temperate, he will probably benefit from being allowed to work up to a good half-speed on the way to the post, run along for a furlong and then gradually slow down before pulling up.

This is particularly important on a cold day. On arriving at the start he should be walked quietly around until called up or his girths are being tested, so that he does not stiffen or catch cold.

It is advisable to keep colts well away from fillies, especially if the latter are in season, so that their attention is not diverted from racing to sex.

There are three methods of starting racehorses: from a barrier, from stalls and by flag, each requiring a different technique.

For a jockey, starting from the barrier is a much more complicated affair than starting from stalls. In the first place, a by no means unimportant aspect is the terms upon which a jockey is with the starter. Though, theoretically, starters should operate without discrimination, the human element cannot be ignored; and a jockey who consistently plays up a starter or is known to refer to him in conversation as a ham-fisted deaf-mute who ought to be a lavatory attendant – or in similar derogatory terms – is hardly likely to get the best of the deal when it comes to the question of the starter letting the field go.

Thus, it is diplomatic to make a point of keeping in the starter's good books. This does not necessitate sending him a case of champagne every Christmas; it is merely a matter of making his job as smooth as possible and, when the starter makes a mistake at the jockey's expense, accepting it is a human error or pointing it out to him good humouredly and politely.

It is also wise to study the methods and idiosyncrasies of individual starters. Some will let the field go when the horses are walking up; others insist on a standing start; a number are inconsistent and have to be played by ear. Some have a particular aversion to jockeys who shout: "Not yet, sir", others tolerate such a plea if justified – as when the jockey is in dire trouble and is sure that the starter is not aware of it.

Occasionally, a starter will give a hint as to when he is going to pull the lever; for example, by the twitch of a facial muscle or opening and shutting his mouth.

The best order of procedure, so I found, was as follows. Having made sure the girths were in order, relax until the starter calls the field up into line. Have as long a rein as is compatible with control, in order to give the horse maximum freedom when he jumps off. Take a quick look up and down the line, to see how the other jockeys are forming up, avoid getting too far ahead of them and arriving at a standstill in front of the barrier – in case it goes up while the others are on the move – or too far behind, resulting in being left.

Have the horse balanced and straight whether on the move or standing still. Keep an eye on the starter for any physical hint that he is going to pull the lever and act on it immediately, thus getting a fractional advantage.

Give the horse full freedom of his head and neck as he leaves the gate.

Shorten the reins to racing length once the horse is into his stride.

In the case of a hard-pulling horse, as Harry Wragg graciously taught me, it is worth getting left a length. This makes it easier to cover up the horse than would be the case if he jumped out of the gate with daylight in front of him. Once covered up, it is usually possible to make the horse race relaxed, without fighting for his head. Much depends on the skill and "hands" of the jockey, knowing the horse, confidence, the way the horse has been trained and his character; but if he has been taught to settle down at home, the chances are that he will do so instinctively on the racecourse once he is covered up.

Having no experience of riding from stalls, I am indebted for the following notes on this art to one of the best exponents among modern riders.

The more at ease and relaxed a horse is in the stalls, the quicker is he likely to start.

A horse should not be chivvied by slapping him down the shoulder and kicking him, since this upsets him and takes his attention off the business on hand.

The nearer he is to the front of the stalls, the quicker a horse will get away. Horses who are really fast beginners from stalls often push their noses right up against the doors. They seem to sense when they are going to open, and if allowed to concentrate their whole attention on the job will break quicker than if the jockey is distracting them by slapping them down the shoulder or kicking them with their heels.

It is essential to get well forward on the horse in anticipation of the start, to ensure being with him as he jumps off; this gives his quarters, which propel him out of the stalls, freedom of action.

Balance is a vital factor. The better a rider is balanced, the quicker will the horse be into his stride.

On horses who have to be covered up, and therefore must not be allowed to get away in front, it is advisable to leave the stalls from the back of them, sitting down in the saddle. This places the rider's weight in such a position as to slow the horse down just enough to enable him to be dropped in behind a neighbouring competitor immediately after leaving the stalls.

The procedure with flag starts is, to all intents and purposes, the same as that with the barrier, except that there is no danger of being hung up. Whatever type of start, always watch the starter's face.

The tactical situation in a race begins to develop from the moment the horses leave the start.

Broadly speaking, jockeys come in one of two categories as regards tactics. Either they are formula-riders, of which Scobie Breasley was a supreme example; or, as Lester Piggott did, they vary their tactics according to circumstances.

Formula-riders are those who adhere to a set plan, regardless of circumstances.

Thus George Duller, an outstanding hurdle race rider between the two wars, invariably went straight to the front and made all the running. Breasley, on the other hand, adopted the principle of waiting towards the rear of the field, keeping to the rails and challenging with a long, late run. Most notable of the few occasions upon which he deviated from this procedure was when, on the orders of the horse's trainer, George Todd, Breasley made the running on that great stayer, Trelawny.

The advantage of riding to formula is that it dispenses with having to make a decision on the tactics to be employed, because this has already been established by the selected formula. Also, as a result of always adopting the same plan, the exponent becomes more expert in putting this particular method into practice than his rivals.

No one among his contemporaries could match Breasley's timing of a finishing run: he could gauge it so that he struck the front only a few yards from the winning post, at the same time gaining a decisive verdict and giving the horse an easy race.

How many jockeys would have had the coolness to take a pull at Santa Claus on entering the straight in the Derby and delay his challenge till the last hundred yards, with Indiana streaking along in front, as did Breasley? He gave his supporters and backers of Santa Claus – me among them – a shock, yet won comfortably by a length.

The disadvantage of formula-riding is that there are occasions when the plan does not fit the circumstances. While Breasley's tactics won him races he should have lost, they lost him some he should have won, because of keeping to his formula when circumstances demanded otherwise.

Those jockeys who vary their tactics place greater demands upon their repertoire than riding to a formula; but in the case of a top-class exponent it is a better system, because it allows the most to be made of all situations.

The disadvantage is that if a situation is interpreted incorrectly, or the necessary actions incompetently carried out, disaster is likely to ensue.

Therefore, when the judgement and skill of a jockey is limited, keeping to a sound formula is probably a better proposition than trying to play it by ear, on the principle that a reliable automatic pilot is safer than a bad human one.

Presuming that a jockey has the ability and confidence to appreciate the tactical situation correctly and take the appropriate action, his first move after leaving the start should be to get the horse in the required position.

If he wants to make the running, he must reach the front as soon as possible. If he wants to wait, he must cover the horse up at once.

In the case of a front-runner, the situation may occur in which an opponent has a similar aim. This gives rise to the danger of "cutting the horse's throat" by racing for the lead, or galloping stride for stride with the leader at an unduly fast pace, which happened to Flamingo and Sunny Trace in the Derby of 1928. Flamingo lasted longest, but had run himself out by the time Harry Wragg brought Felstead with a late challenge to overtake him.

Riding one front-runner against another is a tricky problem, dependent largely upon judgement of pace and the peculiarities of the horses concerned. One thing is certain: whether a horse likes making the running or not, he will never win if he is allowed to cut his throat through going too fast for too long from the jump off.

If a rival front-runner is prepared to share the lead at a suitable pace, a jockey can let his horse run along upsides him until the situation sorts itself out. If after a while he finds his horse moving well enough to take the lead without increasing his pace imprudently, he can move to the front. Should his opponent be going too well for him, he will just have to sit and suffer, hoping that the other horse will crack or give in.

In the case of an opponent going off at an absurdly fast gallop, it is wiser to lie second than to try to lay up with him. The chances are that the horse in front will drop back sooner or later, enabling the lead to be taken over without undue effort being expended.

Naturally, any decision in such circumstances is dependent upon judgement of pace; and a jockey must make up his mind, immediately and accurately, as to the speed at which he is travelling, in relation to the capabilities of his horse, the state of the going, the topography of the course, and the wind. If there is a strong headwind it is advisable to get in behind another horse, so that the latter acts as a windbreak.

Judgement of pace is a matter of experience, sensitivity, concentration, knowledge of the course and understanding of the horse concerned. It may be an innate quality or it may be developed, but without it a jockey is of limited practical value.

In general, racehorses can be divided into two types: those who keep up an even gallop from start to finish and those who can produce a burst of speed over a comparatively short distance.

Most front-runners are one-paced, even if this pace is fast enough to enable them to win over short distances; but a number of horses who like galloping in front are not one-paced, but capable of considerable acceleration.

Horses with good acceleration, amenable to making running, are formidable contenders, because they offer the means of considerable tactical flexibility, whereby opponents can be deluded by variations of pace without the horse expending too much effort.

I used to ride a horse of this category in amateur races, in which he was never beaten. He was a quick beginner and liked to stride along at a very fast pace for the first two or three furlongs. This had opposing riders guessing from the start: they could not decide whether to chase him or wait for him to come back.

After the first two furlongs or so, he would reduce his speed, to give himself a breather. Approaching the final bend – he was an ace at taking corners really fast – he would gradually work up speed again, and by the time his rivals had started to make their challenge in the straight he had gained first run and could not be caught.

His tactical expertise, which he carried out on his own – all that was necessary was to sit still on him – enabled him to beat better horses, who were not tactically employed to the same advantage.

One-paced front runners tend to take a strong hold from the start and pull nothing out at the finish. On such as these a jockey has little option but to sit still and endeavour to prevent them running themselves out before the end of the race. In a finish, more can be gained by holding them together and kicking them out, than by throwing the reins at them and using the whip, since they cannot accelerate and by then either have the situation in hand or are a spent force.

The first move in riding a waiting race is to get covered up. This, as previously stated, is especially important on a puller, as it helps to make him drop his bit or, at least, ease the pressure on it.

The position taken up in the field depends upon the draw, the movements of other horses and the peculiarities of the horse concerned.

The shortest way round is on the rails, except on courses such as Epsom and Brighton, where at one point the track takes a sweep inward and then outward again; so that over this stretch it is necessary to go straight ahead, instead of keeping to the rails, in order to avoid travelling further than is necessary.

It is particularly important to keep as close to the rails as possible when going round bends. Taking bends wide entails losing many lengths.

It is essential that any move during a race should be smooth and gradual, since in this way the smallest amount of the horse's energy is used up.

In any lateral movement, the more gradually it is executed the less ground is given away. For instance, on the straight course at Newmarket, should a jockey decide to bring his horse from the far side to the stands side, he will give away several lengths if he comes across sharply in the first hundred yards or so: but if he brings him across gradually he will lose only a matter of inches.

This was borne out in the 2,000 Guineas of 1949, when Nimbus

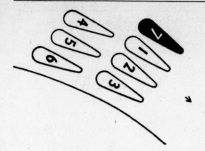

Figure 4.1
Never come round the bend on the outside (like number 7)

Figure 4.2
Though number 7 is in the third rank, he is going the shortest way. When he is in the straight the leaders will break up and he will find a way through somewhere (as in Figures 4.3 and 4.4). Even if he has to move to the outside he will not lose much ground, provided he waits until he is in the straight before doing so

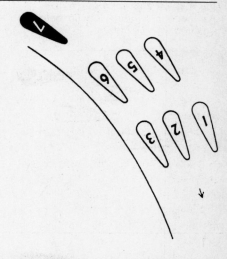

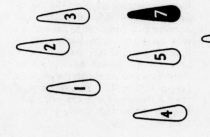

Figure 4.3
From his place in Figure 4.2, number 7 has moved up behind the leaders. He is still on the rails and has not given away an inch

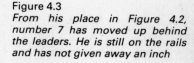

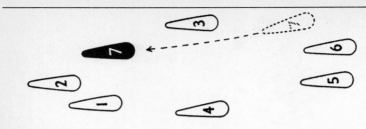

Figure 4.4
Here, the runners have turned into the straight and broken up, enabling number 7 to get through from his place in Figure 4.3, with only one horse inside him

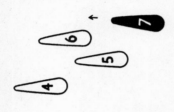

Figure 4.5
Here number 7 is trying to get through a narrow gap on the inside, after turning into the straight. You can do this three furlongs out when you are on a horse who is going well and can quicken, because, if you fail, there is time to pull back and move to the outside, as in Figure 4.7. But if you try to get through on a slow horse, or too near the winning post, you will probably get pocketed

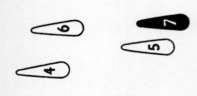

Figure 4.6
Number 7 has been stopped after trying to get through on the inside (as in Figure 4.5). If there was another two furlongs to go and he was on a fast horse with a bit in hand, it would not matter much because he would have time to drop back and come on the outside (as in Figure 4.7). But he is less than a furlong from the post and has no chance of getting out in time

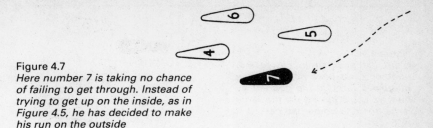

Figure 4.7
Here number 7 is taking no chance of failing to get through. Instead of trying to get up on the inside, as in Figure 4.5, he has decided to make his run on the outside

Figure 4.8
When you have a wall of horses in front of you, avoid getting on the tail of one of them, as number 7 has done, unless you are certain that he is going the best. Otherwise he may drop back, and you will have to snatch your horse up to avoid striking into his heels. Instead, lie about two lengths back (as in Figure 4.9), then you can follow whichever horse goes on and leaves a gap

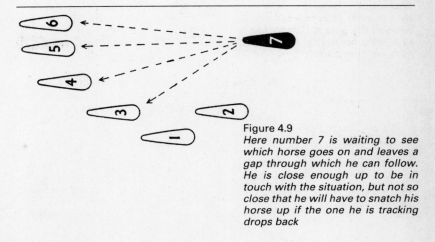

Figure 4.9
Here number 7 is waiting to see which horse goes on and leaves a gap through which he can follow. He is close enough up to be in touch with the situation, but not so close that he will have to snatch his horse up if the one he is tracking drops back

Figure 4.10
From his position in Figure 4.9, number 7 has been able to follow number 5 through the gap left by him. He could have done the same if the horse to go on had been 3, 4 or 6

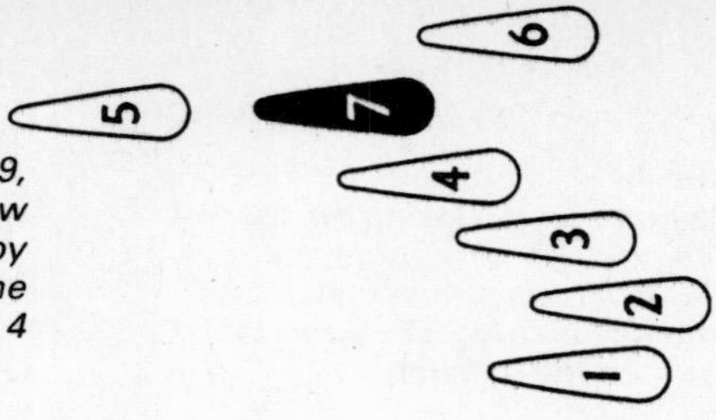

Figure 4.11
When you have only two horses in front of you (like number 7 here), and you are going well, never try and get through on the inside, unless you are certain of getting through. Instead, come on the outside

Figure 4.12
Here number 7 has moved from his position in Figure 4.11 preparatory to making his run on the outside; he cannot get pocketed

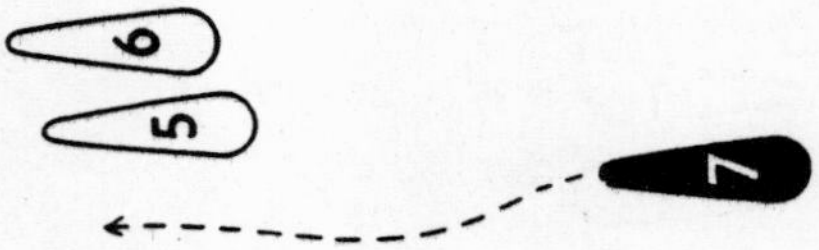

beat Abernant a short-head. Nimbus was drawn in the middle of the field, Abernant on the stands side. Charlie Elliott on Nimbus came very gradually across the course to join Abernant in the last furlong and win by a short-head. Had he come across sharply, the ground he lost would have cost him the race.

Manoeuvres of this kind must be equated with other relevant factors. For instance, if the going along a narrow strip of the course is very much faster than on the rest of the course, the best policy may be to come across to the fast going as quickly as possible, regardless of giving away ground.

Having left the start, the jockey must set about taking up his position. As in all aspects of race riding, this should be done as smoothly as possible, to avoid unbalancing the horse, taking more out of him than is necessary or upsetting him mentally. This last aspect is sometimes overlooked, but it is important, because if a horse's mind is disturbed his attention is not on his job; and a jockey who pulls a horse about here and there, or makes a sudden move without warning, will only confuse and worry his horse.

A horse's position in a race is determined, apart from circumstances, by his individual characteristics. On a horse who is handy and can quicken, there is less risk of getting shut in than on a clumsy horse who has only one pace. Thus, on a handy horse, a place on the rails with no immediate prospect of getting out is a better risk than on a one-pacer.

This is an instance of the advantage of tactics based on circumstances as opposed to those dictated by a formula.

While it is important to take note of how opponents are going, and to mark especially the tactics and progress of the rival which beforehand seemed the chief, if not only, danger, it is unwise to base tactics solely on beating one horse. Many races have been lost this way, through the horse so marked down running below form or being badly ridden, or a disregarded opponent showing unexpected improvement.

A race should be ridden as it develops, not to a preconceived idea as to what might happen.

Formula-riders seldom fall into the trap of riding to beat one horse, because by keeping to a set plan they disregard the tactics of other opponents, whatever danger they appear to represent before the race.

After two or three furlongs, according to the distance of the race, it is usually possible to determine the shape which the race is taking: the speed at which it is being run, the way other horses are going and the tactics of the chief rivals. At this stage, presuming that the race is not a sprint, there is no occasion to become unduly fussed as to one's position in the field. The only place that counts is the winning post.

One of the chief tactical faults among jockeys is becoming anxious at too early a stage in the race. At every stage of the race the jockey should remain completely cool; position himself according to his assessment of the race, regardless of the way his opponents are interpreting it; never ask his horse for an unnecessary, sudden effort, and should manoeuvre himself imperceptibly into a position from which he can launch his challenge at the moment he wishes to do so.

Nothing takes more out of a horse than asking him to keep producing a violent effort during a race. If he is required to move up, he should be asked to do so gradually and on the bit. By dashing a horse from the rear of the field to the front in fifty or a hundred yards, much energy is lost.

At the same time, the point from which a horse's final challenge is made is of vital importance and must depend upon the characteristics of the horse.

The peculiarities of individual horses are an important factor. They must be studied, appreciated and acted upon correctly. For instance, if a horse takes some time to warm up in a race, it is no good hustling him till he is ready to go.

On a horse who does not accelerate quickly, but dislikes making running, it is necessary to start a finishing run further out than on one who can quicken in a few strides. Thus on a horse who does not quicken, it is necessary to start manoeuvring for a challenging position at an appreciably earlier stage than on one which can produce a powerful burst at the finish.

Some horses, while they have to be brought from behind, can only sustain a finishing burst over a short distance. On such horses, it is essential to be placed to challenge so that they need not be asked for a finishing run until they are on the heels of the leaders and the winning post a furlong or less away. To come with a long run from the back of the field is fatal, because the horse has run out of steam before he reaches the winning post.

Before riding such horses I found it a help to walk out on to the course, pace the exact distance of the horse's run, from the winning post backwards, and pick out a prominent landmark from which to start my run.

The characteristic of a short run is sometimes evident in horses who are the result of a pedigree of extremes – and out-and-out stayer on a sprinting mare. One such was Rustom Pasha, by that great stayer, Son-in-Law, winner of the Cesarewitch, Goodwood Cup and the Jockey Club Cup (twice), out of the brilliantly fast mare, Cos, by the sprinter Flying Orb.

Held up for a late, short run, Rustom Pasha could produce a devastating turn of speed and, ridden in this fashion, won the Eclipse Stakes and the Champion Stakes. Ridden otherwise, he was a spent force before the finish.

This is an instance of pedigree proving a guide; and when a horse poses a problem, it is always worth examining his pedigree to see whether it offers any clue to the solution.

Before starting the final run, it is essential to collect the horse, so that he realises what is required of him and is properly poised for the effort. In the profession this is known as "picking a horse up", a term which the layman might find somewhat perplexing.

The importance of picking a horse up before asking him for his finishing effort cannot be over emphasised. It ensures that he is mentally prepared for the effort, is on an even keel and is tensed, like a coiled spring, to unleash his maximum powers. From then on the operation is one of riding a finish.

All tactics are dependent to a greater or lesser extent upon the topography of the course; and it is essential to walk any course which is unfamiliar.

As previously mentioned, lengths can be lost by failing to appreciate features such as the inward deviations of the track at Epsom and Brighton. Equally vital are the contours of the ground on courses where there are slopes or undulations. At Epsom, for instance, there is a steep upward slope from the mile-and-a-half start. Bursting a horse up this can finish his chance in a race such as the Derby, since the effort takes too much out of him, because going uphill requires far more energy than galloping on the flat.

A downhill slope favours a well-balanced horse with good shoulders and forelegs, but one who is straight-shouldered or has upright or unsound joints will be at a disadvantage galloping downhill and is likely to lose ground while negotiating the slope. In the case of such horses it is advisable to be well placed before starting on the descent, to allow for losing ground during it.

It is also advisable to maintain a good steady hold of them to give them every chance to remain balanced until the ground levels out again.

Another important feature of Epsom is the slope of the ground towards the rails after turning into the straight. This has a powerful bearing upon tactics, because it makes horses hang towards the rails, sometimes causing congestion and jeopardising the chance of a horse shut in on the rails getting through. On this account it is advisable to make sure of a clear run in the straight, even if it means moving out from a position on the rails, which on another course could be held with little danger of being shut in.

Another tactical aspect of a slope of this kind is that it demands extra care in ensuring that horses keep straight and do not risk disqualification through coming off the true line, as a result of hanging towards the rails.

On the Rowley Mile course at Newmarket the all-important geographical feature is the Dip, two furlongs from the winning post. Races can be won or lost by tactical use of the Dip.

A horse who excels on a downhill slope can gain a vital advantage through descending the Dip at full speed, thus gathering momentum to carry him out of it and on to the winning post. Whereas, on a horse who comes downhill badly and has to be held up going into the Dip, allowance must be made for losing ground while negotiating this feature.

On courses with a downhill slope into and for most of the straight, notably Epsom and Brighton, where the ground also rises in the final furlong, there is a tendency for jockeys to develop a sense of euphoria, inspired by the speed and ease with which a horse suited to the course makes the descent. This is liable to make them forget about the final ascent to the winning post, on which so often the race is decided.

Time and again, horses appear to have won the Derby at a mile-and-a-quarter, but by the time the winning post is reached are well beaten. It should never be forgotten that at only one place is the race judged – the finish; and on courses such as Epsom provision must be made for meeting the demands of the final uphill slope leading to it.

It is one thing to let a horse bowl down the hill as fast as he likes on the bit, quite another to ride his head off merely because he is going downhill, leaving nothing in him with which to cope with the most vital moments of the race.

The tactics so far discussed, as will have been gathered, are from the aspect of middle distance and staying races.

It may be thought that beyond jumping out of the gate and going all the way, there is nothing to tactics in sprint races. This is not so.

Since a horse can only gallop at his absolute maximum speed for a comparatively short distance, about two furlongs, a sprint is just another race, but run at a much quicker tempo. The same principles apply, but to a much higher powered and more delicately adjusted degree than over a middle or long distance.

A one-paced horse runs his race at a more even speed than one with a power of great acceleration.

The most effective method of exploiting such horses is to let them gradually work up to a speed which they can maintain for the remainder of the journey, in this way grinding the opposition into the ground. The technique requires a high degree of skill in judgement of pace, in relation to all other relevant influences, and a thorough knowledge of the horse's capabilities.

Allowing the horse to go along at too fast a pace is liable to result in his running himself into the ground; by setting too slow a pace he lays himself open to being chopped for speed at the finish.

The longer the distance of the race, the easier it is to make an error of judgement in carrying out these tactics.

Whatever the distance of the race, the tactics employed, or the length of a horse's run, it is essential to pick a horse up well in advance of asking him for his final effort.

This diminishes the danger of an opponent getting first run and, by the same token, places a rider in the position of getting first run if the opportunity of seizing this advantage presents itself.

Getting first run can enable impending defeat to be turned to victory. It lies in challenging before an opponent does so, but at a point from which the horse's run can be maintained up to the winning post.

For instance, in the case of two horses of exactly equal ability, having a finishing run of exactly a furlong, all else equal, the one who challenges first will win, provided he does not start his run more than a furlong out.

There is a very narrow margin between getting first run and coming too soon, but it can make the difference between victory and defeat.

Unforeseen circumstances are always liable to crop up and an effective jockey must be able to cope with them. For instance, as already mentioned, a strong wind blowing against the runners. This gives great tactical scope, in that horses in front have to bear the main force, thus expending much energy.

So, by tucking a horse in behind those in front, a jockey can avoid the main force of the wind and in this way conserve his horse's energy.

The tactical principles expounded above apply to any course, even tight circuits such as those in America, courses with a short run in as in Australia, and Chester, which is almost completely circular and has a run in of only 230 yards. On all these courses a considerable number of winners come from behind, as do many winners over five furlongs, even at Epsom.

5 Use of the Whip

The use of the whip in riding can be divided into four categories: punishment, education, encouragement and guidance.

So far as racing is concerned, punishment and education should hardly ever come into it, because, if a horse is properly trained he should need neither punishment nor education. But in some stables, as in some schools, discipline and education leave more than a little to be desired; while even in the best of both types of establishment not every inmate is tractable and intelligent by nature.

Thus there are times when a jockey may have to hit a horse for corrective reasons, or to make him attend to business.

Should the question of punishing a horse arise, the rider will be well advised to ensure that he can do so properly, without falling off, or call it a day. To attempt the task and end on the ground will render the last state worse than the first; and riding in the prevailing fashion of extremely short stirrup leathers, it is not easy to stay in the saddle when a battle with the horse ensues.

If a horse is to be punished at all, he should be hit hard, well behind the stifle and, preferably, left-handed. If he is merely looking around him, a smart tap on the shoulder, without taking the hand off the rein, should be sufficient to remind him that he is not there for sightseeing, and be unlikely to cause a dissolution of the partnership.

In the case of a well-trained, manageable horse, therefore, the use of the whip is confined to encouragement and guidance.

The damage done by improper use of the whip on the racecourse cannot be overestimated. In this way honest horses are turned into rogues, the spirit of a sensitive one may be broken, and races can be lost through horses being caused to go off the true line, or curl up.

The first principle in the use of the whip in race riding is not to hit horses too hard.

Occasionally, a thick-skinned, indolent horse needs a couple of good hard cracks to bestir him, but for the average horse a couple of taps, or even the mere sight of the whip swinging, is sufficient to make him do his best.

If a horse is to keep on racing effectively, he should not be made to dislike it; particularly, he should not learn to associate pain with the finishing stages of a race. If he is to be hit hard, it is far better to give him two or three good cracks some way from home, when he still has some running left in him, than to do so in the final stages when he is all out. Nothing sours a horse more than to be punished when he is doing his best.

This is proved on the racecourse time and time again, and it is not uncommon to find horses who will only exert themselves when they know that the jockey is not carrying a whip at all; or will run on when the jockey puts his whip down.

That great champion, Sir Gordon Richards, was an outstanding exponent at getting the most out of a horse by only swinging his whip at him, or tapping him lightly; while Scobie Breasley, another who could persuade horses to do their best without hurting them, hardly ever touched a horse with the whip.

The late Ivor Anthony, a top-class trainer both of flat races and jumpers, used to say of jockeys who punished horses with the whip that it was a sign of an unfit or idle rider, because it was too hard work riding horses out with hands and heels only.

One of the worst aspects of races confined to apprentices is that boys riding in them are allowed to carry whips.

It is essential to learn to ride a race without a whip, before attempting to do so with one. The place for boys to learn to use the whip is off the horse – on a wooden saddle horse, a hack or on the ground – not in a race. When a boy has become adept at manipulating a whip off a racecourse, he can start putting the art into practice in races not confined to apprentices. If he is not good enough to ride in such races, he is not good enough to carry a whip.

For a jockey to be considered master of the technicalities of his profession, he should be able to use the whip fluently in either hand. That is to say, carry, produce, swing or hit left-handed and right-handed, and change the whip quickly and effectively from one hand to the other.

For some reason, most horses tend to go left-handed as opposed to right-handed, if they veer off a straight line, hang or whip round. This natural tendency is often accentuated by their being perpetually lunged anti-clockwise when they are being broken, and by a preponderance of riders carrying and using the whip in the right hand.

Other factors influencing the choice of hand in which the whip is used are: the side on which a rival is racing and the slope of the ground.

A horse tends to hang towards another one racing upsides him, and to veer in the direction of the slope of the ground.

Thus when two horses are racing side by side, in order to ensure that each keeps straight, in the ordinary course of events the jockeys concerned should have their whips in the hands nearest each other.

On a course such as Epsom, where the ground is the straight slopes downwards to the left, it is essential to use the whip left-handed. Conversely, when racing took place at Lewes, where the slope was the reverse way, it was more practicable to use the whip right-handed.

These general principles must be related to the behaviour of the horse. Sometimes a horse will hang the reverse way to that which can normally be expected; this will necessitate changing the whip from one hand to the other. Or he may start hanging one way and then the other – I once had to change my whip twice in the straight at Lewes, but for which the horse would not have won.

When a horse is racing between two others, it is a better bet to use the whip left-handed than right-handed, because he is then most likely to run straight.

Knowledge of these factors gives considerable scope for gamesmanship. A jockey racing with a horse on his right can get close enough to him to prevent his rival jockey using his whip left-handed, knowing that if he is tempted to bring it out in his right there is a good chance of the horse hanging away from the whip, bumping him and losing the race on a disqualification.

An honest, resolute horse will probably run straight, whether the whip is used in the correct hand, or not; but it is unwise to take this for granted, especially on a strange horse.

The first art to be mastered in using the whip in a race is that of bringing it from the carrying position to the position of action.

The two most effective ways are: to carry the whip in the opposite hand to that in which it is intended to use it, and pull it out as if drawing a sword; or to twirl is through the fingers of the hand in which it is carried, so that it ends up in the position of action.

Another method is to transfer the whip from the carrying to the active position by an underhand movement, rather like changing gear in a car.

Quite often it is desirable, or necessary, to carry the whip in the hand in which it is going to be used. Therefore a jockey should be proficient in twirling it through his fingers, in either hand, or producing it underhand.

If a jockey wishes merely to show the horse the whip, he can do so by waving it at him in the carrying position. In the days when the standard of technical skill among flat jockeys was higher than it is at present, this manoeuvre was considered as lacking in artistry and professionalism; while to be caught with the whip upside down, in which position it is commonly carried by jockeys in America, stigmatised a rider as no better than an inexperienced amateur.

If a horse is running sluggishly, it may be advisable to give him a backhander, that is to say hit him with the whip in the carrying position, letting it fall behind the stifle.

The first principle of using the whip in a flat race is to let the horse see it, by swinging it for a couple of strides, before hitting him. This gives him a chance to answer to it, by increasing his effort, without being hit at all.

If a horse is hit suddenly and without warning, he may be thrown out of his stride by surprise, or swerve, especially if hit with the whip in the wrong hand.

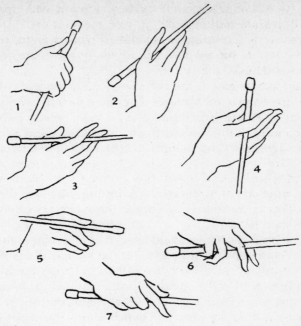

Figure 5.1
Getting out the whip preparatory to using it in the same hand as that in which it is carried

When a horse is hit, the whip should fall behind the stifle; if he is hit in front of the stifle it will cause him to curl up instead of go on.

He should be hit in the rhythm of "swing", "hit", "swing", "hit", so that the whip falls when his legs are curled up under him, thus encouraging him to stretch out to the maximum, a fraction of a second after the blow falls. If he is hit when his stride is at its full extension, he cannot at this stage extend it further.

A horse should be encouraged to run on without being hit if he has answered to the first application of the whip. This does not mean putting the whip down in the heat of battle – unless the horse shows active resentment by not running on – but keep swinging it, without hitting him.

If a horse starts to curl up as soon as the whip is produced or applied, the sooner the rider puts it down and rides the horse out with hands and heels, the better.

The more extravagantly the whip is swung, the more likely is the horse to become unbalanced. The most effective way to use the whip is to swing it parallel to the horse, so that when the horse is to be hit, all that is necessary is to alter the angle of the backswing slightly for the whip to contact the horse behind the stifle.

In recent years a bad habit has become prevalent, namely taking the whip hand off the rein and hitting the horse down the shoulder. This is more likely to make the horse go sideways or backwards than forwards.

One of the practical disadvantages of riding with ultra-short leathers is that it deprives the jockey of the full use of his legs as a means of propulsion. This means that he cannot get the most out of a lazy horse who will not run on under the whip, because he cannot swing the lower part of his leg; any attempt to do so results in grotesque contortions, which throw his body out of balance and hinder rather than aid progress.

Since a remarkable number of horses win when hand-ridden, with their riders sitting still (because they are riding too short to kick), the inference is that it is often more effective to keep a horse balanced and go with him, than to ride him vigorously.

While a lazy horse cannot be made to exert himself except by vigorous riding, many horses resent being kicked out, let alone hit. This emphasises the value of persuading the horse to become a willing partner, as opposed to an unwilling slave.

"Spare the rod" is a precept with which every jockey should be imbued.

It is a mistake to slap the horse down the shoulder while trying to scrub him at the same time. This is often a sign of a jockey being unable to use the whip in one hand or the other, or pull it through.

It is impossible both to scrub in rhythm and slap a horse down the shoulder at the same time, as the latter movement causes a break in the rhythm of scrubbing. The only time to slap a horse down the shoulder during a race is when he is on the bit.

(For further reading on the use, and improper use, of the whip, see the Appendix.)

WARWICKSHIRE COLLEGE OF AGRICULTURE LIBRARY

6 The Finish

The final struggle in a race begins when the jockeys concerned start their finishing run.

As explained earlier, it is essential first to pick the horse up, to ensure that he is prepared for the effort. From then on it is the task of the jockey to persuade, inspire or compel the horse to throw all his resources into attempting to reach the winning post first.

The most important part of the foundation of success in this combined operation is to understand thoroughly the temperament, nature and capabilities of the horse.

It is useless to hit a horse who resents punishment, or to sit quietly upon one who needs driving. Some horses answer to hands and heels, others dislike being kicked out. There are those who will run on gamely under the whip, those who swerve or curl up if the jockey so much as feels for it.

Every horse goes best when he is running balanced and kindly.

Having assessed the horse, it is up to the jockey to ride him out in the way best suited to his characteristics.

The most common fault in riding a finish is to try to "go faster than the horse". That is to say, throw the reins at him, wave the whip and "scrub" (ride him out) at a faster tempo than that of his gallop. This is liable to throw him off balance and make him deviate from a straight line, which might result in disqualification.

In a desperate finish and especially in the case of inexperienced riders, there is a strong temptation to ride with over-enthusiastic vigour. This does not mean that a jockey should merely sit still and leave everything to the horse, but that he should keep in exact rhythm with his stride, whether he is applying all the aids of hands, heels and whip, or is hand-riding him only, and maintain contact with the horse's mouth.

When picking a horse up, the rider slightly increases the pressure on his mouth, at the same time squeezing him, so that he is fully collected for the final effort.

The degree with which such pressure can be applied to the greatest advantage depends upon the nature of the horse. A tough, idle colt will respond to a firm, determined touch, whereas a sensitive, highly strung filly needs tender, delicate handling.

It is one of the arts of jockeyship to be able to handle correctly horses of extreme natures. To go against a horse's nature is to court disaster, though at times the temptation may be acute. The last winner I ever rode was on a horse who resented punishment, and in a tight finish it was difficult to refrain from pulling out my whip and giving him one, but it would have been fatal, as he would have stopped in a stride.

On changing from the state of collection to "scrubbing", it is advisable to increase the tempo gradually, so that it ties up with that of the horse's speed. If a horse accelerates instantly and powerfully, the jockey can increase his own tempo accordingly.

Should the horse respond slowly, the jockey must follow suit by riding him out at the same tempo.

The vigour with which a jockey is riding a horse out does not

Figure 6.1
Starting to scrub

necessarily reflect the effort he is putting into the task, or the effect it is producing.

A loose and unco-ordinated flapping of legs and arms not only is less exhausting than pushing a horse out quietly and powerfully, but achieves less. Jockeys who appear to be doing least are often putting in the most, and vice versa.

The art of riding a horse out in a finish is to preserve perfect contact with his mouth throughout the operation, however desperate the situation, at the same time giving him full freedom of action. The reins should be taut, as if they were bars connecting the bit with the rider's hands, but the horse's freedom of movement should be ensured by maintaining the exact rhythm of his gallop in the movements of riding him out.

It is an extremely difficult art, depending upon ice-cool self-control, a meticulously accurate sense of rhythm and correct poise of the wrists.

On a horse who is going overwhelmingly better than his opponents, it may be unnecessary to move at all after picking him up; but even in such a situation it is dangerous to relax until victory is absolutely assured. Once a horse has been allowed to ease up, it is difficult for him to get going again; and races have been thrown away by jockeys easing up too soon and being passed by an opportune opponent taking advantage of the lapse and coming with a late run, giving the horse who is easing up no time to regain his impetus.

If the horse is running on effectively, hand-ridden, and is master of the situation, there is no point in drawing the whip.

Should the issue be in doubt in the last two furlongs, a decision has to be made as to using the whip. This must depend, first, on the horse's known reaction to its use.

If the horse is not averse to being ridden out under the whip or having it swung at him, the jockey must decide in which hand he is going to use it. This depends upon circumstances; and the jockey should make quite certain that he produces the whip in the correct hand, whether he has to pull it out or twirl it through his fingers. It is better not to use the whip at all than to have it in the wrong hand.

Plates 10 and 11
A comparison between styles of different eras. Bearing in mind that the horse in Plate 10 needed hard driving but would not race under the whip, two questions pose themselves: (1) Would the position of the rider in Plate 11 prove as effective on the horse in Plate 10 as the position of the rider shown there? (2) Would the position of the rider in Plate 10 render him less effective on the horse in Plate 11 than the position of the rider in that picture?

Plate 12
The jockey on the left has his whip in the wrong hand, which cost him the race, as his horse veered away from it and bumped the horse on the rails, who was awarded the race.

Plate 13
A perfect example of the correct use of the whip by the two jockeys concerned in the finish. Each is using the whip between his horse and the one beside him, thus insuring against penalisation for careless riding, should either horse deviate from a straight course and interfere with the other. Each jockey has his horse perfectly balanced, has a good style and excellent contact with his horse's mouth.

Plate 14
The author winning on Pont Cordonnier at Lewes in 1952. His seat is too high off the saddle and contact with the horse's mouth is not complete due to the angle of the wrist being incorrect (compare with the rider in Plate 10); this may perhaps be excused as the verdict was a short-head, gained in the last stride after a long duel.

As stressed earlier it is essential to swing the whip once or twice before hitting the horse. Otherwise, he is liable to swerve or be thrown off balance.

If the horse responds to the whip being swung, there is no object in hitting him. If he does not, the jockey can try giving him a tap and, if he answers sufficiently, return to swinging it.

Should the horse start idling he must be given another tap, if necessary repeating the dose every few strides.

Only in extreme cases should a horse be hit hard, and then the best time is when he is picked up. To hit him hard in a finish will only sour him, unless he is exceptionally thick-skinned and indolent.

Once the whip has been taken out, it should only be put down when the jockey is absolutely sure he cannot be caught. A lazy horse will slow down straight away if the jockey stops swinging the whip, once he has started; and it is only too easy to be caught napping this way.

Deciding whether to ease up or not is a tricky business. A cardinal fault in race riding is to look round, because it tends to unbalance the horse and take his attention off the job on hand; and, unless a jockey is on the rails, while he is looking over one shoulder an opponent may take him by surprise, making his run on the other side.

In general, except occasionally on a front-runner, it should never be necessary to look round. Challenging horses can be seen out of the corner of the eye and heard – unless a jockey is deaf. And if a jockley who is in the lead having come from behind has to look round, the chances are that he has hit the front too soon.

If looking round, only the head should be turned, not the body, as this is liable to unbalance the horse.

There is only one place at which a race is decided: the winning post.

Thus it is extremely important to manoeuvre a finishing run so that once a horse has got his head in front he will keep it there till he is past the post. There is nothing more disheartening to a horse, after he has hit the front, than to have his lead wrested from him.

To gauge a horse's final effort so that he hits the front at the crucial moment in a tight finish is the true art of jockeyship. It depends upon keeping just enough in hand to enable the horse to pull out a little extra, thus getting first run without an opponent realising it until too late.

This sub-divides the stage of riding a finish into taking the horse from the picking up stage to the riding out stage and, while riding him out, leaving scope for the further stage of pulling out a shade more, without opponents realising it is there.

How a jockey does this is a matter of personal choice in techniques.

Gordon Richards would pull out his whip a long way from home and start to swing it, so that it looked as if he was under pressure. But when challenged he would suddenly manage to produce a bit more out of his horse because, though it was impossible to detect, he had left a little up his sleeve.

Others have a quiet style, yet produce the same result.

The best exponent in the use of the whip in modern times is Joe Mercer, who combined controlled vigour with perfect rhythm.

It is impossible to make a horse pull out what is not there, but in the case of two horses of equal merit, the one whose ability is exploited to the best advantage is the one which will win.

Apart from the characteristics of the horse, an important factor is the assessment of the situation with regard to the movements of other jockeys.

Riders who compete against each other regularly get the opportunity to know their rivals' techniques, which should be studied carefully and evaluated, in order to avoid being deluded by them, and to be able to take advantage of their weaknesses.

An aspect not to be overlooked is the deceptive angle of the finishing line on certain courses, most notably Windsor. On such courses, a jockey may be convinced that he has won by half a length or more, but find that the photograph has shown him to have been beaten.

It is essential to leave nothing to chance in these circumstances and on no account to try to win cleverly – by so doing I once risked being lynched at Windsor, through winning by what appeared to be a comfortable half-length on a hot favourite with a stone in hand, when the margin proved to be a short-head.

7 Gamesmanship

With the advent of the patrol camera, television, starting stalls and stricter all-round control, there is little scope for gamesmanship in modern race riding. Had the Derby of 1949 been run in the present era, the odds are that Amour Drake would have got the race. That master of every department of race riding, Charlie Elliott, on Nimbus, having gently guided Swallow Tail virtually into Tattenham Corner Station, imperceptibly but effectively proceeded to take the ground of Rae Johnstone on Amour Drake who, when he finally managed to get a clear run on the inside, only failed to get up by inches. At least, that was my reading of the race and this interpretation is by no means a purely individual one.

Likewise, resorting to more robust tricks of the trade such as elbowing an opponent, locking his leg, putting a heel in the flank of an adjacent horse, holding on to the tail of a rival horse or flourishing the whip in his face, is asking for trouble nowadays.

Such niceties – if that is the right word – of the profession, to be executed without detection must be practised with exceptional skill and delicacy, or in a fog.

By the same token, starting stalls obviate jumping across an opponent at the start, lining up in the wrong position, whipping a horse round at the start on purpose – the only way a subsequent pillar of respectability on the Turf succeeded in stopping a good sprinter in a field of three when, as an apprentice, his employer told him he would break his neck if he won – and so on.

There is, however, a measure of scope for gamesmanship in more refined forms.

Provided a horse does not bump or bore an opponent, there is nothing to stop his rider bringing him so close to the latter that he cannot use his whip properly, or is forced to switch it to the wrong hand and thus run the risk, himself, of deviating from the true line and being disqualified.

Other manoeuvres include: luring an opponent into a pocket and then keeping him there; giving the impression that a horse is beaten when he has plenty of running in him; luring a horse with a short run to hit the front too soon; slapping a boot noisily when racing beside a horse who will curl up at the sound of a whip falling; imperceptibly squeezing or roughing-up a jady filly; and clicking the tongue in the hearing of a hard-puller, to make him take an even stronger hold.

Sometimes, also, there is scope for gamesmanship in the jockeys' room.

In the ears of a rider whose nerve may leave something to be desired, observations in the nature of: "You want to watch that one you're riding; he took his lad nearly to Cambridge before he could pull him up the other day", or: "The top bend's suicide, greasy as hell and sure to bring something down", are not the most welcome of words and may well sow the seeds of over caution. While: "He's a terror to ride for", does not imbue with confidence an inexperienced rider, employed by a trainer for the first time.

The clinically aseptic atmosphere, the computerisation and mechanism of space age racing has certainly put the Turf in a strait-jacket of rectitude as compared with pre-war days, but there is no denying that some of the entertainment has gone out of it as a result.

Conclusion

The chief factor in flat race riding is jockeyship, as opposed to horsemanship and style. By jockeyship is meant judgement of pace, tactics, strategy, coolness, determination, alertness, strength, balance, fluency with the whip, initiative, opportunism, sensitivity and horse-sense.

Horsemanship and style come after. But, all else equal, the best horseman and stylist has the edge on his rival.

The chief fault of modern flat race riding is that insufficient attention is paid to mastering the technicalities of the profession, particularly fluent use of the whip in either hand, and scientific principles are sacrificed to fashion and habit.

There is something wrong when a leading jockey loses a race through overbalancing and falling off, or earns disqualification and suspension as a result of the whip being used in the wrong hand.

There is no scientific evidence that there is anything to be gained by riding with ultra-short leathers, which is the present fashion and merely places the rider in an unnecessarily insecure position and removes the use of his legs as a means of guidance and propulsion.

A rider must mould his style according to his build and, if necessary, modify it to allow for the peculiarities of individual horses. It should always enable him to combine the scientific distribution of his weight with security and efficiency.

The American style of riding differs from that generally practised in England, in that the position of jockeys is more consistent than tends to be the case with English riders. Americans sit closer to the horse and are never seen in violently contrasting positions, whereas in England it is not uncommon to see the same jockey riding in the American style at one time and, at another, sitting upright with his seat down in the saddle.

If a jockey decides to ride with ultra-short leathers he should adopt the American style rather than try to blend it with the English style of the immediate pre-war and post-war eras. That is to say, keep the lower part of the leg rigid and not attempt to kick with it. A rider who tries to combine the two schools is liable to find himself unbalanced, insecure, with his centre of gravity in the wrong place and presenting a grotesque appearance.

Basically it is the horse who wins the race. Sometimes the scale comes down in his favour as a result of good jockeyship, at other times the result goes the other way through an error or judgement on the part of his rider.

The following points summarise the operation of effective race riding:

(1) Find out as much as possible about the horse.
(2) Find out as much as possible about the opposing horses.
(3) Weigh up the probable tactics of the opposing riders. Consider their strong and weak qualities.
(4) Do not reveal your plans to your opponents.
(5) Know the course. If necessary walk it.
(6) Make sure that the saddle and bridle are in order before mounting.
(7) Agree the tactics with the trainer.
(8) Agree on a procedure, should the circumstances make the proposed tactics impractical.
(9) Put yourself on good terms with the horse as soon as you get on his back. Adjust the length of your stirrup leathers according to circumstances – the distance of the race, the going and the peculiarities of the horse.
(10) Set him off calmly and properly balanced to canter down.
(11) Regulate his speed to the post according to orders or the requirements of the horse.
(12) Pull up gradually – never with a jerk.
(13) Endeavour to keep the horse calm and relaxed before going into stalls or lining up. On a cold day, keep him quietly on the move.
(14) Check the girths.

(15) Keep alert in the stalls or when the field is called up to the barrier.

(16) Break quickly or slowly, according to the requirements of the horse.

(17) Give the horse plenty of freedom of his head and neck to enable him to find his stride as quickly as possible.

(18) Ensure that he is running smoothly and balanced before making any tactical move.

(19) Weigh up the situation, taking into consideration: the pace being set in relation to going and wind; your position in the field and that of your opponents; the way the horse is going and eccentricities of other horses and riders.

(20) Decide tactics according to instructions and circumstances arising from (19) above.

(21) Place the horse in the position best suited to circumstances.

(22) Get him running as smoothly and relaxed as possible.

(23) Try to anticipate any necessary changes of position.

(24) Carry out any changes of position as smoothly as possible, avoiding sudden acceleration – the more level a horse's pace until he is asked for a final effort, the less energy will he expend.

(25) Work gradually into a challenging position, so that the horse is not left with too much to do in the final stages.

(26) Time the finishing run to the requirements of the horse: some need to come with a long, steady run, others can only sustain a finishing run at top speed for a furlong, or less.

(27) Once a finishing run is started, go right through with it till victory is assured.

(28) Avoid looking round: the position of following opponents can be ascertained out of the corner of the eye or by slightly turning the head; turning the body unbalances and disconcerts the horse.

(29) Before resorting to the whip:
    (a) decide in which hand it is to be used;
    (b) swing it once or twice before hitting the horse;
    (c) if he does not respond, stop hitting or return to the carrying position;

    (d) if the horse veers away from the whip, change it
immediately to the other hand or put it down and hand-
ride him: it is only too easy to lose a race through not
keeping straight;

    (e) never punish a horse.

(30) In a long battle to the finish, try to keep a little in reserve for
the last few yards.

(31) In a close finish, do not stop riding until well past the post –
some finishing lines are very deceptive.

(32) Maintain contact with the horse's mouth throughout the
race except, perhaps, in the last strides.

(33) Pull up gradually: snatching a horse up after passing the
post can break him down.

(34) After the race, mark any lessons learnt from it: your own
mistakes or those of other riders, the reactions of the horse –
whether other tactics might suit him better, how he moved on
the going, and so on.

(35) Avoid becoming over-confident from success or despondent
through defeat.

(36) Develop a discerning and ruthlessly critical assessment of
your own riding; then, if you are satisfied with your
performance, the adverse opinions of others need cause you no
unrest.

(37) Do not fall off, especially when winning.

Appendix

I wrote this pamphlet, *The Proper and Improper Use of the Whip*, in
1982 and it was published by the Jockey Club. It seems appropriate
to include it here in its original form.

FOREWORD

I have been asked to write a foreword to John Hislop's excellent pamphlet on the "Proper and Improper Use of the Whip in Race Riding".

This subject has been one of considerable controversy in recent years, and it seems particularly appropriate that young jockeys should now have the benefit of expert guidance.

That is why I am so delighted to welcome this excellent pamphlet so ably written by John Hislop with the advice and suggestions of several acknowledged experts.

John Macdonald-Buchanan
(Senior Steward of the Jockey Club)

PREFACE

In general, the use of the whip by jockeys in Great Britain is humane and restrained, more so than in most other countries; but from experience as a Steward at Flat and Jumping Meetings and as a Member of the Disciplinary Committee of the Jockey Club, it has seemed to me evident that on a number of occasions when jockeys have been penalised or disqualified as a result of improper use of the whip this could have been prevented, if the riders at fault had paid attention to the basic principles of using the whip correctly.

It therefore seemed that if a pamphlet setting out these principles were to be made available to jockeys, apprentices and amateur-riders, it might help to keep them out of the Stewards' Room as a result of using the whip improperly.

The pamphlet which follows is based on the teaching of two outstanding tutors of jockeys, Stanley Wootton and the late Tom Masson, and the help and advice given to me during my riding days by eminent, contemporary, professional jockeys, especially Charlie Smirke and the late Charlie Elliott, with both of whom I rode work frequently.

I would like to thank Frenchie Nicholson, Johnny Gilbert, Jimmy Lindley and Council Members of the Jockeys' Association of Great Britain, particularly Lester Piggott, Paul Cook and Steve Jobar, for reading and advising on the original draft which has been amended according to their suggestions.

John Hislop
11 January 1982

THE PROPER AND IMPROPER USE
OF THE WHIP
IN RACE RIDING

Background

For more than three centuries the Thoroughbred has been produced primarily to race. As a result, racing is in his nature and unless he is abused or suffers from some disorder, the average racehorse enjoys his task, is willing to try his hardest and does not need to be punished in order to make him do so.

Occasionally horses are born with an unco-operative nature or are imbued with an undue interest in sex, but these are likely to respond even less to punishment than a willing horse.

When a horse develops a dislike for racing there is nearly always a reason for it. He may have something wrong with him, have been frightened as a result of breaking a blood-vessel, have been raced too frequently on going to which he is unsuited, or be soured by having been hit too often and too hard during races.

An honest horse who does his best of his own accord is likely to resent undeserved punishment, by swerving or hanging away from the whip, or even refusing to race altogether.

Except in the case of lazy horses, there is often no reason to hit a horse in a race at all. It is remarkable how, on many occasions, horses who are falling back under the whip will run on when the rider puts it down.

An intelligent horse associates punishment with the displeasure of his rider and cannot understand why he is being hit when doing his utmost to win.

Technique of Using the Whip

Before attempting to use the whip on the racecourse, a rider should be proficient in handling it. *This can be achieved largely by practice off a horse and takes time, but is an essential part of a jockey's training.*

There are certain fundamental principles in using the whip which have applied throughout racing history.

If these are ignored, the jockey concerned will land himself in trouble sooner or later. He may incur a fine and, or, a suspension, lose an important race or, through having been suspended, be deprived of riding winners, none of which might have occurred if he had observed the said principles.

It is therefore of the utmost importance that a jockey learns how to use the whip properly, thereby avoiding the penalties which he may incur through improper use of it.

*

A recent aspect which has come to bear on the use of the whip in race riding is public opinion, arising from viewers of racing on television, especially members of animal welfare societies. Such opinion is often un-informed and ill-founded, but unfortunately can carry considerable weight in official circles not always favourably disposed towards racing.

Influences of this kind could bring pressure to bear to ban the whip altogether, or restrict its use so stringently that it has virtually no purpose, if sufficient evidence of apparent misuse were to be produced.

This would be detrimental to race riding and on occasions might prove a source of danger, where a horse endeavours to savage another or a jockey.

The Stewards of the Jockey Club are anxious to avoid any such restrictions being forced upon them, and, therefore, intend to take particular care that there should be no cause for public opinion to be exerted in this way.

A jockey should be able to:

(1) Use the whip effectively in either hand, *especially the left* hand, since almost every horse, if he deviates from a straight line, tends to hang, swerve or whip round to the left. *A jockey who cannot use his whip fluently in either hand is not master of his profession.*

(2) Get his whip out quickly both by twirling it through his fingers and by pulling it through with the opposite hand.

The reason for being able to get the whip out by twirling it through the fingers is that if a horse tends to hang one way or the other, the whip can be carried in the hand in which it is to be used.

It is the quickest and neatest way of producing it, at the same time giving the horse a chance to see the whip before it is used in action.

(3) Change the whip from one hand to the other quickly and neatly. This is an essential operation when a horse hangs first one way and then the other.

(4) Return the whip quickly and neatly from using it to carrying it.

To finish with the whip upside down in England is considered a lack of professionalism – in America it is customary to carry the whip upside down throughout a race. This looks ungainly and possibly adds to wind-resistance.

Purpose of the Whip in Race Riding

This falls into three categories: Encouragement; Guidance; Correction.

Encouragement   Covers the use of the whip as a means of making the horse go faster, either by swinging it at him or hitting him.

Guidance   Comprises using the whip to keep the horse straight.

Correction   Embraces the use of the whip to fend off another horse who is attempting to savage a horse or a jockey, or to prevent a horse from doing so.

Causes of Improper Use of the Whip

Improper use of the whip stems from the following main failings:

(1) Ignorance of the nature and psychology of the racehorse.
(2) Ignorance of the correct use of the whip.
(3) Inability to use the whip correctly.
(4) Over-anxiety and, or, loss of self control.
(5) Using an unduly long whip.

Accepted Principles of Proper Use of the Whip

The generally accepted principles of the proper use of the whip are:

(1) First, to decide whether to use the whip at all.

If a horse is obviously winning, is not slackening his pace and there is no imminent danger in the shape of a challenging opponent, it is unnecessary to do more than ride the horse out with hands and heels.

(2) Should a jockey decide to use his whip, he must get it out in the correct hand.

This decision depends on:

(a) the horse having a known tendency to hang to the left or the right;

(b) having a horse racing beside him on one side or the other;

(c) having a horse racing on either side of him.

In the case of (a) the jockey should get his whip out *on the side to which the horse tends to hang*.

In the case of (b) he should get his whip out *between his horse and the horse racing beside him*.

In the case of (c), if the horse has a tendency to hang, the jockey should get the whip out *on the side towards which the horse is known to veer*.

(3) Since any horse is more likely to veer to the left than the right, the rider will be well advised to get the whip out *in his left hand in any circumstances other than that of having a horse racing on his off-side, or his horse having a known tendency to veer to the right*.

(4) Having got his whip out, the rider should swing it two or three times before hitting the horse, to give him the chance to run on without having to be hit. But in such circumstances as a horse trying to run out, prop, savage another competitor or stop at an obstacle, a horse may have to be hit immediately and without warning.

Hitting a horse without first showing him the whip can take him by surprise, throw him off balance or make him swerve.

(5) If the horse runs on as a result of being shown the whip there is no point in hitting him unless a horse draws up to challenge him.

To keep hitting a horse who is running on and is not being challenged is both pointless and can cause the jockey to be penalised.

Sometimes jockeys, especially those without much experience, lose their heads when they strike the front in the straight, going for the whip and hitting the horse to the finish. *This practice will inevitably land a jockey in trouble.* All that is necessary is to ride him out with hands and heels.

(6) *To punish a horse who is obviously beaten serves no good purpose and comes into the category of improper use.*

(7) If after being hit several times – two or three as opposed to six or seven or continuously – a horse does not respond, there is no point in keeping on hitting him. The chances are that he cannot or will not pull out any more, and further punishment will be of no avail. If the horse does not respond, it is important to ride him out vigorously with hands and heels, especially if there is a chance of finishing in the first four. If he does respond, he should be encouraged to keep going by the jockey swinging the whip at him or by riding him out with hands and heels.

(8) When a horse hangs or swerves away from the whip, the jockey should put it down at once. Then, either pull it through to the other hand or ride the horse out with hands and heels only.

Interference caused by failure to observe this principle comes into the category of careless riding and is likely to incur a penalty.

(9) A horse should never be punished severely. Hitting him hard and continuously is more likely to make him curl up than go faster and may inbue him with a dislike of racing.

This practice will be penalised.

An exceptionally tough horse may survive a limited dose of this treatment, but will be none the better for it and may not require it in any case.

(10) Save in exceptional circumstances, such as a horse attempting to savage another or a jockey, a horse should never be hit anywhere other than behind the hip-bone or down the shoulder.

Hitting a horse in the stifle or on a testicle can cause great pain and is unacceptable.

(11) Some horses mark more easily than others, and the fact that

a horse is not marked does not necessarily imply that misuse has not occurred, if there is evidence that he has been hit continuously.

(12) Lazy horses may need a slap with the whip when they are picked up, and several more at intervals, in between having the whip swung at them, to keep them going if in danger of defeat in the run it.

This does not mean that it is permissible to hit them continuously and hard.

Such horses sometimes respond to the whip being changed from one hand to the other, especially when the jockey has started with the whip in his right hand.

Lazy horses can also be driven out by vigorous use of a jockey's legs.

Interference caused by Improper Use of the Whip

In all too many cases of interference, the basic cause has proved to be that the offending jockey has *had his whip in the wrong hand, most commonly the right hand instead of the left.*

This fault will always weigh against a jockey in an inquiry and may mean the difference between a verdict of accidental interference and one of careless riding.

A jockey who observes the guide lines set out above should never give cause to be penalised, or lose a race on an objection through improper use of the whip.

BY THE SAME AUTHOR

Steeplechasing

From Start to Finish

The Turf (Britain in Pictures series)

Of Horses and Races

Far from a Gentleman

Anything but a Soldier